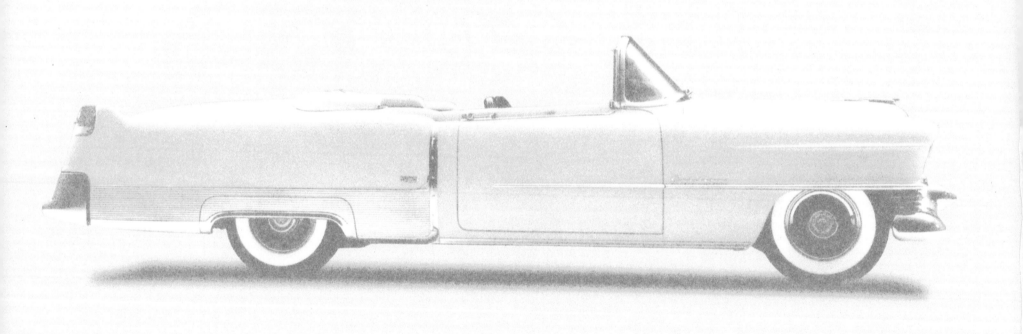

Design copyright ©
Carlton Publishing Group 2003
Text copyright ©
Jonathan Glancey 2003

This edition published in 2003 by
Carlton Books Ltd
A Division of the
Carlton Publishing Group
20 Mortimer Street
London
W1T 3JW

A CIP catalogue for this book is
available from the British Library.

ISBN 1-84222-942-7

Project Manager: Stella Caldwell
Editor: Peter McSean
Designer: SMITH
Picture researcher: Steve Behan
Production: Marianna Wolf

THE CAR

A HISTORY OF THE AUTOMOBILE

JONATHAN GLANCEY

JONATHAN GLANCEY IS
ARCHITECTURE AND DESIGN
EDITOR OF *THE GUARDIAN*.
A FREQUENT RADIO AND
TV BROADCASTER, HE IS
AUTHOR OF *THE STORY
OF ARCHITECTURE* AND
CARLTON'S BEST-SELLING
C20TH ARCHITECTURE. A
JAGUAR FAN SINCE THE DAY
HE FIRST SAW ONE OF THE
LAST NEW MK2s HOWLING OUT
OF A LONDON SHOWROOM, HE
HAS ALSO OWNED AND COPED
WITH A VARIETY OF BRITISH
CLASSIC CARS. HE LONGS
FOR AN ASTON-MARTIN DB4GT.

INTRODUCTORY ESSAY

A

A

EGYPTIAN WAR CHARIOT

Faster than fairies, faster than witches;
if not quite as fast as the sky gods, this
was the way to travel 3,500 years ago:
ecologically sound, lightweight,
reliable, fast, and with plenty of fresh
air...what more could any living god
want?

B

LOVE ME, LOVE MY CAR

Are these chaps waking her up or
putting her to bed? Either way, we tend
to cherish the car more than we do our
families, loved ones and animals.

C

TAKE THIS!

Henry Ford was in no mood for
pleasantries when he set about one of
his cars – not because he detested it,
but because, in this case, he wanted
to prove how tough it was.

A

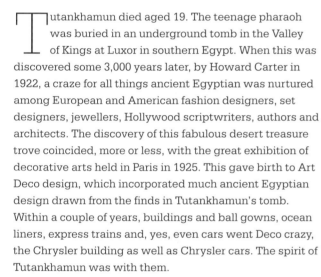

Tutankhamun died aged 19. The teenage pharaoh was buried in an underground tomb in the Valley of Kings at Luxor in southern Egypt. When this was discovered some 3,000 years later, by Howard Carter in 1922, a craze for all things ancient Egyptian was nurtured among European and American fashion designers, set designers, jewellers, Hollywood scriptwriters, authors and architects. The discovery of this fabulous desert treasure trove coincided, more or less, with the great exhibition of decorative arts held in Paris in 1925. This gave birth to Art Deco design, which incorporated much ancient Egyptian design drawn from the finds in Tutankhamun's tomb. Within a couple of years, buildings and ball gowns, ocean liners, express trains and, yes, even cars went Deco crazy, the Chrysler building as well as Chrysler cars. The spirit of Tutankhamun was with them.

And yet, for all their fancy dress, many Art Deco buildings and very many Art-Deco-adorned automobiles were less sophisticated in a number of engineering ways than six very special machines found by Carter in the Valley of the Kings a little over 90 years ago. These six machines were Tutankhamun's war chariots. The first time I saw them, some time in the late 1980s, in Cairo's magnificent Egyptian Museum, I was as dazzled by their construction as by their decoration. Not only did the chariots appear to be brand new, but they were distinctly modern in a way that Colin Chapman, founder and designer of Lotus Cars and its lightweight, nimble, sporting machines, would have appreciated thousands of years on. True, my first impression was that these evidently rapid machines were the Ferraris of their day; or Ferraris as if styled by Versace. Yet the more I gazed at them, the more I came to look beneath the surface gilt. And, now, I know – courtesy of a number of American academics – that Tutankhamun's chariots really were high-performance machines. Aside from ultra-lightweight superstructures, they boasted lubricated, long-life bearings, tunable, semi-independent suspension, multi-layer tyres, a structure designed to withstand bending and twisting, and spoked wheels that would have given these machines and their riders an exceptionally stable ride. With just 2hp up front, the chariots would have been faster than any competitors. Written records testify to their success in battle.

So here were high-performance machines of their day that, in certain ways, were more sophisticated than an Art Deco Chrysler, for all its beefy engine, pneumatic rubber tyres and plush, sofa-style seats. I remember thinking on that first encounter with Tutankhamun's chariots that I would have preferred to get around by these machines at the turn of the twentieth century than by one of Henry Ford's first cars. They would have been faster, more reliable, more efficient in energy use, kinder to the environment and infinitely more stylish.

That day, I had come to the museum, in one of those awkwardly stretched Mercs you find across the Middle East, from the pyramids at Giza, buildings infinitely more refined and sophisticated than many of the Post-Modern blunders blighting the world's cities in the 1980s. To say the road was busy was like saying Harrods sale is a bit of

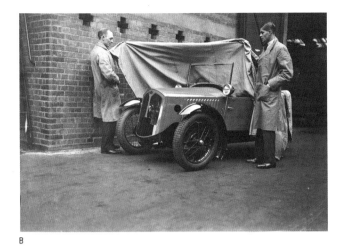

B

a crush. Overladen lorries, smoking coaches, pick-ups of every kind sashayed in a drunken dance along the die-straight avenue that leads from Giza to Cairo. Between them, donkeys borne down with panniers, rib-thin horses pulling carts at a trot, occasional camels, mad dogs – and this Englishman. It was very hot. A donkey pulling an abusively heavy cart collapsed in front of my cab. The driver, in full view of his family and the crawling traffic, jumped down from his seat and began lashing the pathetic beast mercilessly with a cruel whip.

I jumped out and, after a brief discussion, clocked the driver, and rested the animal's head in my lap. Water was brought by a moved, or guilt-ridden, coach driver. The police arrived. I was accused of assault. I was, it has to be said, ashamed of my aggression – I am normally a mild-mannered fellow – but my side, thankfully, was taken by the crowd. The donkey, foaming at the mouth and shaking violently, gave a huge sigh, and expired. I unhooked reins that been digging into what flesh covered its old bones. The cart it pulled had all the

sophistication of a 1970s Morris Marina: slow, resisting, uncomfortable, wobbly, hard to steer. The animal had been forced to work much harder per kilo carried than the lithe war horses that would have raced Tutankhamun along antique roads and across ancient dunes.

Several thoughts crossed my mind. Would the pugnacious cart driver have beaten a pick-up if it had broken down on the Giza Road? Would he have run it on tyres inflated with about as much air as a canary carries in its tiny, trilly lungs? Might he have paid attention to the gauges on the dashboard of his vehicle and noticed that something was awry? He clearly didn't notice – but, then, I suppose, he didn't care – that his donkey was labouring fatefully and in danger of imminent collapse.

Yes, John Cleese, in the guise of Basil Fawlty, the enraged hotelier star of the classic BBC TV comedy "Fawlty Towers" did thrash his BMC 1100 when it failed to start at a time when he most needed it to save his professional skin, but relatively few motorists are as idiotic as Basil Fawlty or as stupidly cruel as my Egyptian

cart driver. Like you, I have witnessed people who wax, polish and T-Cut their cars even as they kick the dog, curse the cat, and generally abuse their families.

Why is this? Because the mechanically propelled vehicle, and most of all the car, is a tin god, and one of our own making. Since its invention proper in the 1890s, in Germany and France, the car has been worshipped like no other machine. More temperamental than a Hollywood star, greedier than a Wall Street financier, dirtier, when all is said and done, than a pig rolling in mud, and more destructive than a fireworks factory in a thunderstorm, the car is a curious bedfellow. Today we find it almost impossible to live without it. We fuss over it. Talk about it proudly in pubs. We build it little houses to live in. It is truly part and parcel of our lives, every bit as necessary to us as dogs were to Stone Age hunter-gatherers and settlers alike. Or horses to young Egyptian kings.

Car factories themselves are becoming increasingly like places of worship, or art galleries, which are much the same thing. Just look at Volkswagen's latest glass

C

F

HORSELESS CARRIAGE
It took a while for the car to develop an aesthetic all of its own. It is easy to imagine horses pulling a handsome, craft-built carriage like this.

G
THE PROMISE OF FREEDOM
The car promises more than it can ever really deliver; where can you drive a car like this E-Type, as it was designed to be driven? In your head, in your dreams.

F

Tutankhamun's day, included the nimble, lightweight, war chariot.

Oxen, llama, camels, yak, donkeys and other beasts of burden performed, and still perform, the work of today's lorries and vans. Only horses, though, could really get us going fast. But a fast horse is a pedigree creature; it has never, except in military and certain nomadic societies, been a form of transport for the common man, much less woman. Speed, then – which along with the notion of independence, is the great attraction of the car, as opposed to a lorry or van – was a mercurial realm in which only the rich, their favourites, or the gods might have the opportunity to play.

Even when the first cars emerged, coughing, spluttering and frightening the horses little more than a century ago, they were sluggish things. Almost any horse could outpace every one of the earliest horseless carriages. In any case, these comical-looking gadgets had none of the beauty or elegance of line, much less the dignity of a pedigree horse. And it was to be very many years, as this book shows,

before the car developed an aesthetic of its own, separate from that of the horse-drawn or railway carriage.

The first challenge had been to find a reliable and lightweight means of motive power that would allow an automobile to out-distance a horse. Several well-recorded experiments were made over the centuries, even the millennia, with forms of steam power.

Five hundred years before Christ rode a donkey into Jerusalem at the height of his human fame, Hero of Alexandria demonstrated a steam turbine. It was much admired, but no one really knew what to do with it. After all, what was the point of a steam-powered warship when a man and sail-powered trireme or quinquireme could go as fast as anyone needed to go at the time? Facts which had made sea-going, horse-worshipping ancient Athens a regional superpower? Which king would have needed so much as a steam pressure-cooker in an age when he could engage legions of slaves to cater for his every whim?

Moving quickly on, which eighteenth century king, queen or emperor would have wanted to travel by

Cugnot's ungainly steam carriage? This clumsy brute hissed, smoked, generated dirt and, in any case, had a top speed, in a short sprint, of 4mph. Even a silken princess at the court of Versailles could move faster on her own two dainty feet.

The car proper finally emerged with the development of the internal combustion engine. This was at a time when expresses on Britain's railways were well able to run safely and smoothly at 90mph and could cover long distances, with handsome dining cars and lavatories, at the rate of a-mile-a-minute. It took those first faltering cars some while to catch up with steam expresses, but when they did, they promised to change the face not just of public transport, but of the world.

Once its reliability was proven, the car spelt freedom. Of course, it took the development of motor roads, enduring tyres, petrol stations and workshops to help it on its way, but soon enough it was spinning all day, every day, the length and breadth of continents, a machine for all seasons and purposes. As this book shows, the car blossomed to become an integral part of our lives. It changed the face of roads and the housing and architecture that grew up alongside these. It created the motorway, the garage, the petrol station, motels, shopping malls, drive-in cinemas, much of suburbia, and traffic jams. It helped police and criminals alike. It gave us drive-by shootings and the armoured car. It gave us reels of Hollywood cop movies and car chase sequences. It became a prop for film and TV stars. It gave horses a race for their money as grand prix circuits flourished. Above all, it became both an inevitable form of transport and a highly desired status symbol.

We all know, though, that the freedom Henry Ford promised us is unreal. It might be real, kind of, if you happen to live in rural Montana, the heart of Canada, in the middle of Australia or in a Germany still free of a maximum speed limit and where cars are engineered so thoroughly, expensively and well because they really do get driven, day-in, day-out, at sensational speeds. For the rest of us, though, the quality of our car, the state of our roads, laws or sheer congestion conspire to slow us down, hem us in. There may be nowhere to park once you have left home. It might well be better to commute by crowded commuter train than by car, yet millions of drivers still set out each morning from their homes in the knowingly mistaken belief that today's journey will be better than yesterday's, that, somehow, the tide of traffic will part as miraculously as the Red Sea did for Moses, and that we will drive heroically, speedily and unimpeded just as smooth-looking models do in cinema and TV ads.

Oddly, this really did happen to me one day. I was driving a brand new V12 Sovereign from Jaguar's Browns Lane factory back home to London. Whichever way I nosed this silent saloon, the main roads were choc-a-bloc. I turned off the first minor road I could and threaded towards Banbury to look at the fine Neo-Classical church at the top of the hill there, and for a cup of tea and Banbury cake, before riding, fresh like a cock-horse, on my rural way. I made a turn when no other car turned and the road seemed to disappear. It was a Friday early evening in June. I threaded the big, sure-footed car through strange chicanes. There was no traffic. And suddenly before me was a great open road without a single car, much less a donkey and cart or king's chariot, anywhere in sight. Cautiously, I launched the Jag down on to this miraculous freeway, and opened her up. Fifty, sixty, seventy miles per hour. Nothing. Just an unimpeded sweep of uncannily smooth concrete. I crested the brow of a hill. Still no other road user in sight. Summer swifts darting and a hovering kestrel above, but absolutely nothing on the road. I was off. Foot sunk gently but deeply into the Wilton pile and the big-hearted car gathered speed like Concorde on its way (no more, sadly) from Heathrow to JFK. Down the hill I peaked out, "maxed" the car as they say in machismo real men's car mags (along with "stump-pulling torque" and other gym-pumped terms). The speedometer read 150mph, the rev-counter needle haunted the red mark on its dial. Sheer, Toad-like bliss. I eased up comfortably in time to see barriers across the end of my secret, dream-like road. I steered off through more curious

G

cogs and chains, topped off with radiators, hoses, spinning turbochargers, whistling superchargers, heating ducts, batteries and all manner of gizmos and eccentrics. The last may or may not refer to the owner.

Only enthusiasts delight in getting their hands oily, while service mechanics are paid through the nose to do so. To the majority of owners, the way a car works is increasingly the stuff of Byzantine courts: secret, inscrutable, ineffable. Significantly, too, few manufacturers this side of the sporting or machismo enthusiasts' market sell their cars on their technical specification any longer. Advertising is concerned with being, first, clever and ironic, and, second, with "lifestyle", that improbable string of brands and labels we are meant to hang around our supposedly sophisticated necks to prove just how smart, cool, with-it, discerning and wealthy we are. But, actually, just a bit naive and all too willingly taken in by hype.

Recently, I got to drive one of those funny, upright little Audi A2s, a breed of mechanical terrier, that I took to like a duck to a gamekeeper's gun. It has a panel that you can lift to top up the radiator, should you ever have to. Owners need never look at the engine, wherever it is, ever. Engines in older generations of cars were designed not to be ignored but to be looked at and admired. The engine cowlings of Rolls-Royces, Mercedes-Benzes, Hispano-Suizas and those of other grand, double-barrelled machines were designed to open up at the side, so that the great motors, all shining brass, steel and aluminium, could be revealed in all their might and magnificence. These were engines that appeared to have had more in common with the great workings of *The Flying Scotsman* or the *Queen Mary* than with modern cars, ashamed of their venerable mechanical underpinnings. In a digital age, who cares for pistons and connecting rods?

One of the great delights of cars built before the electronic and digital ages is that everything in them is as free from power assistance and digital gizmos or, in other words, as genuine, straightforward and somehow as right as possible. I have to be careful here. I don't mean sit-up-and-beg Ford Prefects or any number of slow and creaky cars no more sophisticated than the Mamod steam engines with which I filled the house up with saturated steam, spitting oil and the strangely intoxicating fumes of methylated spirits as a child, but the likes of Mercedes 540Ks, Bugatti 35Bs, Deusenbergs and Bentley Speed Sixes. Those cars had an honesty about them, a mechanical sincerity and, by our standards, an engineering other-worldliness. Having had the chance to drive these machines, each has been a revelation. The Bugatti remains sensational, an all but peerless racing car in the 1920s, a very fast car today, as sensual to pilot along the road as a Spitfire is in the sky.

As for safety, things have changed, and very much for the better. And yet, there is something sad, if not sane, in the loss of motoring innocence. The joys of sitting on fathers' knees as they smoked untipped cigarettes, quarterlight windows open, and you steered and changed gear, and asked, politely, if you could go a hundred, are very much gone. Unquestionably seat belts, airbags, power-assisted steering, powerful brakes, children's

L

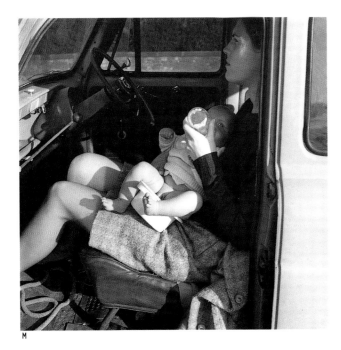

seats, speed limits and other devices inside and outside the car have saved many lives. Perhaps little Joshua and Jessica are a lot safer being driven to expensive nursery schools two miles down the road in a Mitsubishi Shogun, Range Rover or Jeep Grand Cherokee protected with bull-bars than walking or taking the bus or train, where at least every second filthy, disease-infested seat is taken by murderers, molesters, pyschotics, perverts and other penny-dreadful tabloid monsters.

A couple of years back, I witnessed a fascinating cameo of two families at play on the wonderfully blustery and unspoiled beach at Holkham in North Norfolk. Three bright and beady local children were playing with their boisterous mongrel. They were barefoot and barely dressed even though it was cold. They were having great fun. They happened to run back to the car park at the end of the beach's long boardwalk as I jogged back with my dog. Dad, in T-shirt and jeans, was reading a tabloid paper behind the wheel of a sand-flecked Toyota pick-up. "In yer get," he hollered without looking up. Up bounced the dog,

in clambered his playmates among the various boxes in the back of the van, and off they went chattering and barking into rural Norfolk. Perhaps a passing safety inspector or policeman would have had a fit. I do not know. In any case, my attention was drawn to a sobbing boy, of much the same age as the Toyota gang, dressed in layers of posh rain-proof clothing and brand new wellingtons. He was being strapped tightly into a rear-facing child's safety seat of an air-conditioned, top-of-the-range Jeep by a no-nonsense smokey-blonde matriarch with a voice that could be heard in the neighbouring county. Her beefy, expensive husband looked on gloomily. After much ordering about and many tears, the vault-like doors of the go-anywhere four-wheel-drive vehicle, an essential for Britain's upper-middle classes faced with the infamous and treacherous Himalayan landscape of East Anglia [in truth, all but as flat as a pancake, and as gentle as a labrador retriever napping on a summer evening after supper], were sealed and off they went, unhappily but safely, on their way to an important lunch.

I know which car I would have preferred to be in as a child, but, yes, motoring in the paranoid, safety-conscious, litiginous developed world has long lost its innocence. It is not often fun. It is a duty, if not a chore. This loss of innocence is, I feel, shown throughout the pages of this book. When we selected the pictures, we found ourselves facing a barrier – raised somewhere in the 1980s – when images appeared to become luridly coloured and almost consistently commercial, in an aggressive and humourless sense. In them, no one seems to be enjoying themselves. At the same time, the cars themselves changed considerably, becoming smooth, peardrop-shaped, global, aerodynamic and absurdly "organic', designed to cause the least offence to the greatest number of people worldwide. Or awkwardly, and insincerely, "retro". Gone were national characteristics, idiosyncrasies and innovative design. Regulations in the motor industry are partly the cause of this, yet the more we ploughed through reams of pictures, the less we liked what we saw from the 1980s onwards. This is not entirely due to nostalgia, but

N

N
1939 FORD PREFECT
The quintessence of a "nice drive"; a
basic family car that smells of
petrol chugging off to the seaside
for fishpaste sandwiches and
lashings of ginger beer.

O
1962 CHEVROLET IMPALA
In biographies, we rarely hear
about the cars famous politicians of
the past drove; JFK was US
president when this Chevvie
cruised Washington avenues.
Which power-broker might it have
belonged to?

N

because of the way the motor industry, our relationship with the car, styling and photography itself have gone.

I very much like the lack of irony in these old pictures, the sense that the car, for all its mechanical gaucheness and lack of real sophistication, was seen as an adventure on four – and, occasionally, three – wheels. I liked very much looking at snaps of quite ordinary families marking many of the key events of their lives with proudly owned cars in the background. True rites of passage. I liked the idea of a "nice drive", perhaps especially because I was brought up to think, without condescension, that such things were a nonsense. A drive, no matter how brisk and stylish, was a means of getting from one particular place to another, but only at certain times. Long distances were best travelled by train. Cars might ride on low-loader railway wagons on very long journeys, where they might be welcome at the other end, or nosed gently into the pot bellies of Bristol freighters to be airlifted to the Continent. My Uncle Reg, a one-time tea planter from Assam, Eighth Army officer and, in later life, engineer for Vauxhall at

Luton, was just about the only person who ever took us for "a drive". Even then, it was brief and designed to show us a new model, Detroit-style Vauxhall or otherwise, to explain the workings of some new engine. My curiosity was insatiable, but I never wanted to go on a "nice drive". Fellow schoolchildren spoke of long, hot, sickly drives in sticky cars reeking of petrol and bound for Pembroke, the Cornish Riviera, the Lakes or even Scotland. They would be stuck in tortuous tail-backs on even more tortuous roads. The Pembroke Coast, Cornish Riviera, Lakes and Royal Scot expresses, meanwhile, roared past proudly on metalled tracks.

In putting the book together, we trawled through our own cupboards and drawers fetching out forgotten family snapshots. It is remarkable just how often cars feature. They are used to mark out our lives. Here we are as babes in arms, then school children on summer holidays, with Mums and Dads, dogs, Uncles and Aunts, and those distant cousins and family friends that, try as you might, you can never put a name to. I see these family

photographs abandoned all too often in antique markets and car boot sales and wonder who all these smiling people are staring out at us so optimistically and standing in front of cars. We may not know who the people are, yet we can still recognize the make, model and even the date of the cars. Look at the Ulster family on page 11. I do not know their names, but I can spot, like you, a Rover 2000 hiding behind those natty clothes and smiling faces. And, we can divine from a picture like this some of the aspirations of those who liked to be snapped in front of the chic Rover.

Throughout the book, we have largely selected pictures to show people – whether owners, drivers, film stars or models – with the cars; this is because the car is designed for people and without them it is as lifeless as Tutankhamun's chariots are locked away in the Egyptian Museum in Cairo. Well, not quite lifeless. The best car designs do express a latent energy, so much so that we can't wait to get behind the wheel and zoom off, fueled on the particular dream this or that car promises.

O

A rocket-sled ride in a Monteverdi Hai, a Devon lane bumbling in a Hillman Minx.

What this book tries to show is how cars have become inextricably linked with so many aspects of our lives, including fashion, sex, politics and cinema. This is not a conventional car book, although I think it was meant to start out that way, because although I am fascinated by the history of the automobile and have a great fondness for certain cars, their engineers and designers, I am intrigued by the way they are used as props in our everyday lives. And, equally, how they are so often missing from, say, biographies and studies of the famous. You might imagine from all the millions of words written on Stalin or Che Guevara that they were strangers to the car. But here we see Stalin, the Soviet Union's "Man of Steel" clearly thrilled by his new armour-plated Zis limousine. And how incongruous it is to be reminded, if not here, that Che Guevara, the seemingly ascetic revolutionary hero, drove himself, badly, away from his second wedding in Havana, to fellow soldier Aleida March, soon after the Cuban

revolution in 1959; the car was a lurid, bright green, fan-tailed Chevrolet Impala. It rests today in the national motor museum in central Havana. I was shocked, although of course I shouldn't really have been – sometimes a car is just a means of transport, after all – when I first saw this blowsy capitalist plaything. I had imagined that Che would have driven Aleida away in a Jeep. That, of course, is American, too.

This book is a snapshot of these things and not, in any way, a comprehensive account of the social, and much less, the engineering history of the car. The subject is daunting and there are many fine books on individual marques, designers and engineers to keep you researching till the last drop of oil has been drained, profitably, from the deserts of the Middle East, and new types of machines, whether hydrogen-powered, hovering or virtual, or whether donkeys, bicycles and chariots take over when our mad love affair with the car ends. The odd thing is that if this was to happen, it would begin in the developed world. While we might yet gallop along lanes

bright with birds, shaded by trees, on super-lightweight chariots, the poorer peoples of the world will be stuck in fuming jams in characterless cars, as they are today in Bangkok and Guangzhou. I look through these pictures, and for all the glorious cars I have driven and owned, the fascinating conservations I have had with engineers and designers from the late, great Wally Hassan – of Bentley and Jaguar fame – to today's young turks at the Royal College of Art in London, I can't help wondering where on earth we've ended up. I envy Tutankhamun's freedom as he rode chariots far more refined than our commonplace cars, with their oily, whirry engines and noxious emissions. Then I remember he died at 19, and that, as yet, we cannot turn the clock back. Even with this thought in mind, I find myself called back to the growl of a Mk2 Jaguar's exhaust, the whine from its Moss 'box, its flickering Smith dials, the deep-growl of Wally Hassan and co's big-hearted straight XK six, the hiss of its SU carbs, the promise of the freedom of the road, in real style and until the next jam.

THE HORSELESS CARRIAGE

1

THE HORSELESS CARRIAGE

1
1885 BENZ

This is one of the world's very first cars, a pretty, lightweight buggy designed by Carl Benz – there he is, looking pleased with himself, in front of the new car's front wheel – from the ground up as a petrol-driven machine. The engine was a single-cylinder 1.6-litre device producing some 3 or 4 hp, allowing the Benz to ride at up to 8mph. Drive was by bicycle chains; these broke on this very first run. Benz, born in Karlsruhe in 1844, built his first four-wheeler in 1893. He shares the honour as the inventor of the car with his fellow countryman Gottlieb Daimler. The companies they created merged in 1926, when Benz was still alive, to form the mighty Daimler-Benz organization.

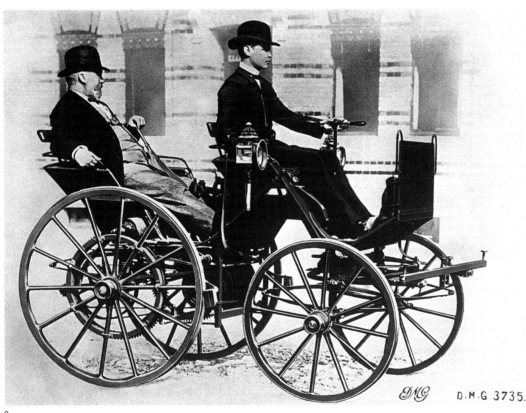

2

2
1886 DAIMLER

Here's the other original car designer and maker, Gottlieb Daimler, born in 1834, being driven by his son, Wilhelm, through the streets of Berlin in the world's first four-wheeler. The car, which looks every inch a "horseless carriage", was powered by a free-revving engine designed and made by Wilhelm Maybach, another formidable figure in the development not just of the car, but of the aero and other engines, too.

3
1896 FORD QUADRICYLE

Henry Ford at the tiller of his very first car. It had no brakes and no reverse gear, but it did have four wheels, an electric warning bell, and it went, more or less. Ford was 32 at the time. His mass-production empire was some years in the distance, but he was on the move, and without horses.

3

4

4
1899 DE DION BOUTON
Ah, monsieurs, which way are we going? The push-me, pull-you look of the 3.5hp Vis à Vis (face to face) De Dion Bouton. Georges Bouton is at the wheel. The science of ergonomics was clearly in its infancy. The car, though, was well engineered and formed the basis of most De Dion cars until 1908.

5
1901 OLDSMOBILE
Production of this handsome, 7hp single-cylinder car ran from 1901 to 1907. It cost $650. The curved dash and slightly, at least, boxed-in bodywork gave the car quite a racy look. It was still easy to imagine a horse pulling it, but the aesthetic of the car was emerging, if slowly.

6
1901 BARON DE ZUYLEN'S SPECIAL
How many moustachioed, boatered and toppered Frenchman can you fit in a vintage car? This is Baron de Zuylen, Comte de Dion, president of the Automobile Club of France, and his contingent at the finish of the 1901 Paris-Berlin automobile race, in his early estate car. You would have needed at least four horses to pull this mighty motorized cart.

5

6

1904 FLINT BUICK

This is Walter L Marr, Buick's chief engineer, and Thomas D Buick, son of the car maker David Dunbar Buick, arriving back in Detroit on a test run from Flint in their prototype car in 1904. Compared to the boys across the road with their bicycles, these pioneering motorists are filthy. The horse looks the other way from the car, as the horse was increasingly to do.

1906 STANLEY STEAMER

Locomotives for the road, the extraordinary cars of twin brothers F E and F O Stanley from Newton, Massachussetts, were among the very fastest of their day. They took a while to start up – 30 minutes – but once they got motoring, these comfortable and quiet cars were hard to catch. This is the 1906 model at some speed on an English rally in later years. The 1908 30hp

Speedy Roadster was capable of more than 60mph, while in 1906, the Stanleys took the world land speed record in at 127mph in a sensational, low-drag, cigar-shaped racer. Its two-cylinder, 3.1-litre engine was provided with steam by a boiler pressed to a very intense 1,000lb per square inch. Steam, for a while at least, was king on the road as well on the rails and the high seas.

7

9

9
1907 BUICK MODEL D
David Buick was born in Scotland. He was taken to America when he was two and eventually became a bathroom plumber. He began making cars in 1902, but sold out to William Durant and the nascent General Motors just six years later. The tough-looking 1907 model featured Buick's first four-cylinder ohv engine. The company established its works racing team that year.

10
1906 BUICK
Ox cart gives way to horseless carriage on a Michigan bridge. These oxen would soon enough be replaced by a Ford pick-up.

11
1909 ROLLS-ROYCE SILVER GHOST
One of the first truly refined cars, the Silver Ghost was a fine machine that could run far, fast, smoothly and reliably. This car is powered by a six-cylinder 7.4-litre engine. Could it fly! Actually, the two severe-looking men on board in bowler hats will be the judge of that. They are Orville and Wilbur Wright, pioneers of powered flight. The Hon C S Rolls himself is their distinguished chauffeur. Rolls died in a flying accident in Bournemouth, Dorset in 1910. His aircraft was a Wright Flyer.

10

THE HORSELESS CARRIAGE

11

16
1921 PEUGEOT QUADRILETTE
Peugeot's 60km/h baby car brought the horseless carriage to thousands of people who thought they would never be able to own a horse, or even a donkey, much less a car.

17
1926 MODEL-T FORD
Going where no horse can go... a Model-T as a snowmobile. It was the Model-T's ability to outdo the horse even on its own territory – the farmyard, if not the race-track – that encouraged American farmers to give up the horse and turn to cars, pick-ups, tractors and trucks.

18
1920s MODEL-T FORD
Well, here's another fine mess... Stan Laurel and Oliver Hardy caught between two Los Angeles street cars in a sequence from *Hog Wild* (James Parrott, 1930). The Model-T was used and abused in films like no horse ever should or could be. Its comic potential was well established by the 1930s.

16

17

FASTER, FASTER...

19

20

21

19 + 20
1904 FIAT 75HP

Vincenzo Lancia (1881–1937) was a big man in every way. Choosing not to become an accountant, he took up engineering. He was with Fiat in 1899 at the very beginning. Giovanni Agnelli made him Fiat's chief test driver and a member of the Fiat race team. Known as the "Red Devil" for his great speed at the wheel of the blood red Torinese cars, he set lap records but won few races because of mechanical troubles. He did win the 1904 Florio Cup, however, two gruelling laps over a 370km course on dusty roads from Brescia and back via Cremona and Mantua. His average speed was a sensational 115.7km/h (71.88mph). Try that in a modern 75hp Fiat today. Lancia stopped racing in 1906 and founded his own car company with Claudio Fogoli the following year. It is now owned by Fiat.

21
1901 MORS 60HP

The winning cars line up at the end of the 1901 Paris to Berlin race. First over the line, in 15 hours 33 minutes and 6 seconds, was Henri Fournier at the big wheel of a 10-litre 60hp V4 Mors. Second and third place went to the two Panhards on the right. The drive chain on the big Emile Mors racer broke just as Fournier was about to set off on a victory run. Top speeds were up to 75mph at this time.

22
1909 BLITZEN BENZ

Victor Hemery at the helm of the record-breaking four-cylinder Blitzen Benz (Lightning Benz) at Brooklands race track in Surrey. He had been timed at 125.95mph, taking the world speed record from Fred Marriot, who had reached 121.57mph in a Stanley Rocket, a steam car, at Daytona Beach in 1906.

26
1913 PRINCE HENRY VAUXHALL
Laurence Pomeroy trained as a
locomotive engineer before joining
Vauxhall in 1905. In 1910 he
entered Prince Heinrich von
Preussen's "tours" – a high-speed
German rally – with a three-litre
model. This led to the four-litre
Prince Henry Model. With 75hp,
it was smooth, if not quiet, and
capable of a very relaxed 60mph
cruise and a top speed of 75mph.
For its period, it was a very
accomplished machine, and
a big success in trials and rallies.

27
1921 VAUXHALL 30/98
A 4.5-litre E-Type Vauxhall at full
tilt, throwing up dust at a speed
trial. These events were immensely
popular between the two world
wars, allowing amateur drivers
to try their luck and risk their
necks. The Vauxhall, designed by
Laurence Pomeroy (1883–1941),
who trained, like W O Bentley, as a
locomotive engineering apprentice,
was one of the finest sporting cars
of its time, even though it was
based closely on the Prince Henry
Vauxhall, dating from 1913.

28
1932 MG J2 MIDGET
Not exactly quick in absolute
terms, but there was immense fun
to be had seeing how quickly you
could get your new sports car up
a muddy hill without sliding off or
getting stuck. This is a delightfully
English scene at the Abingdon
trials, Oxfordshire, in 1932. The
chaps squeezed into the tiny
cockpit wear their caps at jaunty
angles while the bloke in a cap
sitting on the ragged stone wall
gives them a disapproving look;
call that a car, you nonces. In fact,
the J2 (1932–34) was a fine little
machine. Although its 847cc
engine was only good for 65mph or
so, what it did, it did in great style
and was a delight to drive. It gave
many people their first opportunity
of trying out a real sports car.

26

27

29

29
1924 BUGATTI
Not to worry, old chap, the jolly old
wheel's gone and dropped off. This
is Raymond Mays, the renowned
English racing driver, looking
wonderfully unconcerned as he
loses a wheel at speed from his
Bugatti. Ettore Bugatti, the great
car designer and maker, had been
so impressed by Mays's trouncing
of land speed record-holder
Malcolm Campbell on the Shelsey
hill climb, that he gave Mays one
of his cars for free. Some gift. The
unflappable Mays went on to help
create two legendary British racing
marques, ERA (English Racing
Automobiles) and BRM (British
Racing Automobiles).

30
1915 DUESENBERG
Bill Chandler at speed in one of the
great American cars on the new
Des Moines Speedway, Iowa, on
August 7, 1915. The cars lapped at
more than 90mph – the track lived
up to its name.

31

31

31
1937 ROLLS-ROYCE PHANTOM III

A magnificent Park-Ward-bodied 7.3-litre V12 Phantom III sets the pace at Aintree, in the wet, in 1937. The car boasted independent front suspension adapted from a General Motors system. Built from 1936 to 1939, it was comfortable, drove well and, for such a big car, was quite quick enough. In October 1936, *Autocar* recorded a top speed of 92mph, 0–60 in 16.8 seconds… and an overall fuel consumption of just 10mpg.

32
1935 TATRA 77A

Austrian engineer Hans Ledwinka's streamlined masterpiece, the exquisitely engineered rear-engined, air-cooled six-seater V8 Tatra was revealed to an astounded public in 1934. Ledwinka had teamed up with fellow engineer Erich Uberlacker and Hungarian aerodynamacist Paul Jaray to shape this revolutionary 140km/h machine. The 1935 model boasted many modifications, including a larger 75hp 3.4-litre, and a top speed of 150km/h. The Ledwinka streamliners were much prized by German army officers after the annexation of Czechoslovakia by Nazi Germany in 1938. A number were killed driving too quickly; the Tatra was fast in a straight line, but a handful around corners. The army banned its use.

33
1939 LAGONDA V12

Here is one of Britain's finest pre-war cars, the Lagonda V12, engineered by W O Bentley, in racing guise at Le Mans, 1939. With its lightweight aluminium body and extensive use of alloys, the great 230hp 4.5-litre car was fast. Almost unmodified from the stock 100mph road model, the two Lagondas (you can just see the nose of the second one here) entered for the 24-hour race came in third and fourth. The cars rode well and were equipped with all-synchromesh gearboxes – rare before World War Two – and powerful hydraulic brakes. They remain a joy to drive more than 60 years on.

FASTER, FASTER...

34
1937 MERCEDES-BENZ W125
These mighty Mercedes were fully capable of 200mph. Designed by the young Rudolf Uhlenhart, who could all but match the German racing team's top drivers, the car was equipped with a 646hp twin-overhead-cam, four-valves-per-cylinder, supercharged 7.7-litre V8. Here is one the cars taking off in the 1937 British Grand Prix at Donnington. This race was won by Bernd Rosemeyer in a rival C-Type Auto-Union.

35
1950 ALFA ROMEO TIPO 158
Whether the cars are going forwards or backwards – as it appears here – the Monaco Grand Prix remains of the one of the highlights of the racing year. The tight circuit weaves through the streets of the tiny principality of Monte Carlo, the cars driven at seemingly impossible speed. This is Juan Manuel Fangio, generally considered to be the greatest racing driver of all, on his way to winning the first Monaco Grand Prix in 1950. That year, "Alfetta" drivers – the "little" supercharged 1.5-litre Alfas, timed at up to 192mph elsewhere, were essentially pre-war designs updated for the early post-war international races. At the end of the 1950 season, the Alfa team came home first (Farina), second (Fangio) and third (Fagioli).

36

1954 MERCEDES-BENZ W196

A poster celebrating the 1-2 win of Fangio and Kling at the 1954 French Grand Prix. This was Mercedes-Benz's triumphal return to GP racing, the first time in fact since 1939. Alfred Neubauer, 1930s' team manager, was back in place. His cars were the beautiful W196 streamliners, their 257hp 2.5-litre eights screaming up to 8,500rpm. These are among the very best looking of all racing cars, and were very effective, too.

37

1956 LE MANS RACERS

Rain did little to dampen the enthusiasm of the 250,000-strong crowd as they cheered on the entrants of the 1956 Le Mans 24-hour race. At that time, the drivers had to sprint to their cars before roaring off towards the famous three-mile Mulsanne straight and attaining mercurial speeds. An Ecurie-Ecosse D-Type Jaguar won the race, with a works Aston Martin DB3S and Ferrari 625LM in second and third places. The winning average was 168.122km/h, with the fastest lap at 186.383km/h set by Mike Hawthorn (sixth place) in a D-Type Jaguar. Le Mans remains one of the most charismatic and best loved car races.

OVERLEAF

38

1949 BRM V16

Breaking the sound barrier. Veteran Bugatti, ERA and BRM driver Raymond Mays negotiates the great British workman – on bicycles – and parked Vauxhall Victor, VW Beetle, BMC 1100, among others – on the occasion of a gathering of the Club International des Ancien Pilotes, July 17, 1967. Actually, this is probably a later model, because the cars were made and raced up until 1954. Although powered by ingenious 1.5-litre V16s, the BRMs proved unreliable and won few races. The sound they made was unforgettable, though.

39

1969 GP RACERS

Cars scream past photographers and spectators sitting and standing right beside the track at the 1969 French Grand Prix. This seems all but impossible from the safety-conscious vantage point of 2003. For the record, the race was won by Jackie Stewart in a Matra-Ford at 157.251km/h.

FASTER, FASTER...

FASTER, FASTER...

40

40
1965 LOTUS-CORTINA MK1

Jim Clark, the "Flying Scotsman", lifts a wheel of his white and green-striped Lotus-Cortina at Brands Hatch in 1965. Clark was among the all-time racing greats, and the souped-up, twin-cam Cortina one of the delightful surprises of 1960s motor racing. It seemed as if anyone could have a go. But, even if they could afford the Lotus-developed Ford, would they ever get to drive this well?

41
2003 CHIP GANASSI RACING HAVOLINE DODGE

US muscle cars zooming around the California Speedway at Fontana, CA. The occasion is the NASCAR Winston Cup Auto Club 500 race on April 27, 2003 and Jamie McMurray leads the pack in a Dodge. The cars, like most contemporary racers, are plastered in corporate advertising. They can lap at more than 180mph.

42
2003 FERRARI

This is Michael Schumacher, the great champion German racing driver of the past decade, refuelling during the 2003 Malaysian Grand Prix at Kuala Lumpur. By this time, not only had GP racing, originated in France, gone global, but the cars could be serviced in a matter of just a few seconds at pit stops. This needs to be seen to be believed. The smartly uniformed mechanics resemble worker bees droning around their Queen. Or King, in this case, although Schumacher came sixth in race, yielding first place to the Finn, Kimi Raikkonen driving a McLaren and lapping at an average of 201.629km/h.

FASTER, FASTER...

2003 NASCAR WINSTON CUP VIRGINIA 500

Like a giant Scalextric slot-car circuit… but these are real muscle cars bunched together at great speed. Crowds worldwide never seem to tire of watching brightly coloured cars going round and round. They have done so now for a century. This is a scene from the Martinsville Speedway, Virginia, April 13, 2003.

EVERYMAN

EVERYMAN

44

1924 MORRIS COWLEY

Standing at the side of a damp London street when fairly new, this four-seater Morris was a sturdy, mass-produced product from William Morris's Oxford factory. Morris, born in Worcestershire in 1877, started out as a bicycle maker, like so many early car manufacturers. He built his first car, the Oxford, in 1913. The Cowley dates from 1915 and was progressively developed over the next 15 years. Its distinctive rounded radiator encouraged its nickname, the Bullnose Morris.

45

CITROEN B12, 1925

André Citroën (1878-1935) preferred a playboy lifestyle to tinkering with engines, like most of the pioneers of motoring. However, he possessed, aside from good taste and a fine intellect, a flair for publicity and for shaping popular taste. His first small car, the 856cc Type C Cloverleaf of 1922, might have been cheap, yet buyers could specify a glamorous torpedo-shaped body, while, in defiance of Henry Ford whose methods he adopted, the cars were only available in canary yellow. The B12, a handsome 1.5-litre four-seater, saluted here by an impeccably dressed monsieur, was Citroën's first steel-bodied design.

46

AUSTIN SEVEN, 1922

Here are some 1920s flappers up for a lark in and astride their baby Austin. The "Chummy" – it certainly was – was designed in Sir Herbert Austin's billiard room at Lickey Grange, his country house. The principal draughtsman was 18-year-old Stanley Edge. He took his inspiration from the Peugeot Quadrilette and Bebe models. Priced at £165, the 696cc open-top car sold slowly at first but, with a 747cc engine from 1924 and many other modifications and body styles over the years, it became popular with both the wealthy as a runaround (it was the Mini of its day) and the ordinary families for whom it was conceived. It was replaced by the Big Seven in 1937.

45

46

47
1935 CHEVROLET SUBURBAN
Family, dog, servants – the revolutionary Suburban could carry the lot. This was the very first SUV, a genre so popular with American families and gangsta-rappers today. The Suburban featured a steel body on a half-ton truck chassis, three rows of seats for eight people, a tailgate and strong performance from its 90hp motor. One of its successors carried me safely from Amman and across the length and breadth of Saddam Hussein's Iraq in 2002. I have reason to be grateful to this American automotive legend.

48
**1940 OLDSMOBILE
STATION WAGON**
When this house on wheels was launched, station wagons accounted for just 1 per cent of the US car market. Manufacturers and buyers alike thought of wagons as commercial vehicles. This Oldsmobile marked a sea change in the type's fortune. Not only was it practical, but it had a lively performance from its six-cylinder, 230 cubic inch, 95hp engine and was made easy to drive with the option of Hydra-Matic (automatic) transmission.

49
**NANTUCKET BEACH,
JULY 4, 1925**
As many cars as people. This is the famous Ohio resort in the days before parking restrictions, and at this date, such a scene could really be found only in the United States; the car had taken off like hot cakes.

47

48

EVERYMAN

EVERYMAN

51
1959 DKW UNIVERSAL
A happy post-war German family camp with their rare, semi-streamlined, three-cylinder, 900cc estate car. Throughout the 1950s, European manufacturers worked up dozens of ingenious economical family cars. DKW was originally founded by a Dane, Skafte Rasmussen, in 1916 to make steam cars (hence the name, Dampf Kraft Wagen). The first production cars, using petrol engines, were built in Chemnitz from 1928. DKW was absorbed by Auto-Union in 1932. Refounded in the 1950s, it ceased production of its charming cars, including a miniature Ford Thunderbird lookalike, in 1968.

50
1956 FIAT MULTIPLA
Used as Roman taxis, family runarounds and commercial vehicles, the Fiat Multipla was a cleverly engineered miniature minibus, or MPV (multi-purpose vehicle). Designed, off the back of the baby Fiat 600, to carry six people – in practice many more – it was ideal for the sizeable Italian family of the 1950s. Ingeniously packaged to maximize interior space, it was also great fun to drive.

52
5 A.M., SEPTEMBER 3, 1967.
STOCKHOLM
Here are the Swedes changing over from driving on the left to driving on the right. Quite why it has been so important for the vast majority of the world's nations to drive on the right remains a mystery, especially to the British and Japanese. Does it really make any difference?

53
1935 VOLVO PV36 "CARIOCA"
Only 500 of these striking and technically advanced streamlined Volvos, designed by Ivan Orberg, were made between 1935 and 1938. But here is proof that the makers of one of the world's most endearing and enduring people carriers, the Volvo, have been able to produce glamorous as well as universally acclaimed workaday cars. Volvo is Latin for "I roll"; the PV36 rocks, too.

54
NEW YEAR'S EVE, 1974.
CHAMPS ELYSEES.
CITROEN 2CV.
Mechanical genius, and a symbol of France for 40 years, the 2CV was one of the most remarkable and original cars of all. Designed by the brilliant André Lefebvre – engineer of the Citroën Traction Avant and, later, the DS – the original brief for the TPV (Toute Petite Vehicle) was for a lightweight car capable of driving across a field with a basket of eggs without breaking a single one. Developed from 1938 to 1948, and sold at first in just one colour (grey), it was a huge and enduring success. One of the truly great cars.

53

54

55

55

1961 MORRIS MINOR
Here's the one millionth Morris Minor being inspected at the end of the Cowley production line. Designed by Alec Issigonis, of later Mini fame, the much-loved jelly-mould-shaped car was produced from 1948 to 1971. It remains very much a part of the British roadscape more than 30 years later.

56

1956 RENAULT DAUPHINE
Palatial thoughts after a drive in a true people's car. The Dauphine, the automotive equivalent of a goldfish – have you looked one in the gills, I mean grille (or lack of one) – was produced from 1956 to 1968. Powered by a 32hp 845cc engine mounted at the back, it was a spritely performer, and a very proper four-door saloon. It was originally to have been called the Corvette, but for obvious copyright reasons, the name was changed; and it was never that fast, even when tweaked for racing by Gordini.

57

1962 SUNBEAM RAPIER MK3A
A handsome car from Rootes that did well in rallies, the Rapier was a sporting saloon, made from 1955 to 1967, from a company best known for mass-producing American-style post-war saloons. This one boasts disc brakes up front, a free-revving 1596cc engine and side windows that disappear into the bodywork. The Rapier marked the beginning of the end of austerity economics in Britain; motoring could be fun again.

56

58
1948 TATRAPLAN

This is one of the smaller of Tatra's glorious, streamlined, fin-tailed, rear-engined saloons. The original sci-fi-style Tatras were designed by the inventive engineer Hans Ledwinka in the mid-1930s. Ledwinka had also built prototypes of a people's car similar in concept and looks to the Volkswagen before Porsche unveiled his people's car some years later. The economy model T600 Tatraplan, engineered by Julius Mackerle, was powered not by a mighty, air-cooled V8 as the most famous of these legendary Czech models, but by a 50hp, 1.95-litre four. It was smooth, stable and very quiet.

59
1956 WARTBURG ESTATE

During the Russian invasion of Nazi Germany, the BMW factory at Eisenach was taken over by the Soviets. Post-war, it continued to make BMWs under the name EMW. Finally, in 1956, the old models were replaced by a new marque: Wartburg. The cars were quite big and practical but relied on smoky, two-stroke engines. They were always a bit of a laughing stock in the West, bought by left-leaning families fond of camping, sandals and suspicious politics. This 1956 estate was available with either a 37hp 900cc or 50hp 992cc motor.

60
1965 MOSKVITCH 412

Production at the newly designated MZMA (Small Car Moscow Factory) began after the Great Patriotic War (1941–45) with a pre-war Opel Kadett copy dubbed the Moskvitch, or Muscovite. The 412 shown here was the staple Moskvitch of the 1960s and into the 1970s. Simple, crude, rugged and very easy to maintain, the 1.5-litre car won few friends in the world beyond Brezhnev's; but they were much valued in the former Soviet Union. Here, an heroic young proletarian beauty has bought her Moskvitch some lovely flowers.

58

59

61

61
1937 SKODA POPULAR

Skoda was long considered a joke outside the former Communist Block until its revival by Volkswagen in the 1990s. But, in fact, the Czech company has a long and distinguished history. The 1937 995cc Liduska, or Popular, model was a fine and handsome little car; it adopted contemporary American looks in 1939.

62
1970 SKODA 110R

The 1970s was a tasteful decade, East or West, as you can see in this picture. The car, a fastback, sporting, rear-engined, Czech model, is actually remarkably good fun to drive; a kind of Porsche 911 for everyman. The girl in the picture certainly looks impressed. The five-speed car boasted 62bhp and a top speed of 140km/h. The 110R was successfully raced and rallied. The most powerful version – there was just the one – had an alarming 697bhp, a real sting in the tail, and recorded 348km/h on an autobahn outside Berlin.

63

63
1966 WARTBURG KNIGHT
Here's the new 1966 353 model built at the former BMW works at Eisenach. The body was light and bright, but the mechanics were based on a separate chassis. The engine, as before, was a sturdy, three-cylinder, one-litre two-stroke. Still, our fashionable *frauleins* seem happy with their new people's car. Production of this model ceased in 1976, and of all Wartburgs in 1991.

64
1973 FORD CORTINA MKIII
Well flash, my son, but what are you doing visiting some crumbling old half-timbered pile when you could be flash-harrying down to the yacht club at Burnham-on-Crouch in your brand new – and most probably bronze – 2000E Cortina? This loud, brash Cortina made its debut in 1970. It was very '69 Dertroit, with its Coke bottle styling, acres of chrome, recessed instruments and generally aggressive stance. It was good to drive, simple, reliable and sold like pints of lager in an Essex pub. Since the Second World War, Britain has straddled US and European culture; in the case of the MkIII Cortina, it was Uncle Sam all the way, although without V8 muscle.

65

66

65
1965 FIAT 850 COUPE
A smart, miniature, mass-market "GT". This is the Fiat 850 of 1964 rebodied stylishly by Centro Stile Fiat – the company's in-house design department – and given some extra oomph with a 47bhp, rather than a 37bhp, 843cc rear-mounted engine. A delight to drive and capable of 140km/h, this was Fiat at its 1960s best.

66
1968 FORD ESCORT TWIN-CAM
Ford could produce some very fine sporting cars when it set its corporate mind to it. The Ford Escort MkI was the first car from Ford Europe, a merger of Ford UK and Ford Germany. The highly successful sporting version shown here had a 110bhp Lotus-Ford 1,558cc twin-cam four squeezed tightly under its bonnet. The car was good for 115mph and behaved extremely well. Just 1,200 were made before production ceased in 1970. The Escort itself went on for years to become one of Britain's most popular cars.

1960 RELIANT REGAL MKVI

Look, we can bury it over there, have our picnic and go back up to town by train! Gosh, can we, mummy? I don't want to be sick over my new surfboard again. The first of these bubbly three-wheelers went on sale in 1952. They were improved several times during the 1950s, although all retained the tiny, side-valve, 747cc four-cylinder engine that had first powered Austin's baby Seven in the 1920s. Well equipped and well made, the Regal was regarded fondly, although this family would surely soon be dreaming of a new BMC 1100 or Ford Cortina. Reliant, founded in 1935, went on to build many more three-wheelers, but it also produced the conceptually brilliant Scimitar GTE from 1968, a 120mph glass-fibre GT estate that won it many new friends, including Princess Margaret. Regal indeed.

68
1965 MG MIDGET

Often advertised with clueless dolly birds clutching the gear stick or handbrake, the Midget was a classless, affordable sports car. It was at its prettiest here in the mid-1960s.

69
1968 MERCEDES-BENZ
300SEL 6.3
One horse power meets 250hp
in the guise of the 300SEL 6.3
saloon favoured by racing drivers,
rock stars and discreet business
executives. The clever thing about
this genuinely fast V8 Mercedes
is that it was, and remains, so
gloriously discreet. Remove the
badges at the back and it could
be a much humbler machine
altogether. Mercedes had a
genius for building cars that might
serve – and for years – as taxis,
family hacks or the intercontinental
mounts of professional racing
drivers, and yet all look much the
same, except under the bonnet.
One of its favourite advertising
slogans of the 1960s was "a car
your son will inherit". Add
"daughter" today, and not too
much has changed, although
Mercedes saloons have lost the
almost commonplace look they
once had that made them, almost
if not quite, a part of the crowd.

70
1985 FORD ESCORT USA
C'mon, sugar, please come for a
ride in my Ford Escort. Gee, Brad,
I'm sorry, I just met a guy with a
Bond Minicar ... Enough said.

1978 FORD CAPRI 1.3

Go on, Stan, push it harder, will yer? And, Kevin, you can stop being sick in the back before I give you a good slap – have you heard me? Bleugghhh… sorry, Mum. A bottom-of-the-range 1,296cc Capri getting a push-start (or is he just tanking it up with four-star?) in a smart English service station. The Capri, first launched in 1969, was a Mustang "personal coupe" for the British and German markets. It had a reputation for being a mount for wide-boys but, in fact, it catered for a wide range of tastes and incomes. A 1.3 like this MkII model (1974–78) was positively mild mannered compared to the 3.0- and 3.3-litre beasts that were available. Production of the Mk III Capri ended in 1986. Although named after the Italian island, the car was always called a "Ca-pree" rather than a "Cap-ri" in Britain. It was that kind of motor, mate. So don't come over all fancy on me.

72

1969 DODGE CHARGER

"By the time we got to Woodstock/ We were half a million strong… We are stardust /We are golden/And we've got to get ourselves /Back to the garden…" sang Joni Mitchell, although she didn't add "…and this Dodge Charger out of the mud, man". Woodstock was the biggest pop festival yet. It wasn't quite as beautiful as it was cut out to be, as you can see from this snap of youngsters trying to get their Dodge back on the road. Hey, how much money did these Love Generation, no-possession kids have? That Charger's brand new, man.

73

1999 HINDUSTAN AMBASSADOR

This Calcutta street scene would have changed little since the Hindustan was first made near Calcutta in 1948. At one time in the 1980s, virtually every new car built in India was this 1948 Morris Oxford modified slowly over the years for Indian driving conditions and the ways of crowded Indian cities. This example is adorned for a wedding. The cars, India's Model-T Ford, are very much still in production, although in recent years the venerable BMC B-series engine has been replaced by a smoother, 75bhp, 1.8-litre Isuzu unit. Ambassadors are now seen on the streets of central London in the guise of Karma Kabs, adorned with flowers and smelling of incense and petrol.

POWER AND POLITICS

76
1915 PEUGEOT ARMOURED CAR

It's okay for the chap on top hiding behind the bullet-proof shield and the machine gun, but the driver and co-pilot have nothing except their waxed moustaches to scare off les boches. Brave boys indeed. Armand Peugeot, founder of the car division of this venerable French company - it began making windmills in the eighteenth century when Napoleon Bonaparte was still a corporal - died that year.

77
1916 MODEL-T FORD

Here's the IRA in flat caps ready to take on all comers. No attacking from the front, mind.

78
1936 FORD V8 PILOT

Take that, copper. A posed shoot-out on the mean streets of Depression-era England. The policeman has a bullet-proof window to shoot over. The villain is unwisely standing directly in his line of fire. Ideally, he should be racing away in his 90hp V8 Ford. Few of these sold in Britain before the Second World War; the Pilot made a strong comeback after hostilities ceased. They were popular, like Mk2 Jags in the 1960s, with police and thieves alike.

76

77

78

79
1958 VOLGA

A car much favoured by the secret
police and security forces in the
former Soviet Union and other
Eastern bloc countries. They had
a delightfully sinister appearance.
Powered by strong 2.4-litre fours,
they are slowly becoming collectors
items. Volgas remain in production.

80
1965 ZIL

These enormous cars produced
for top Communist party officials
and, since 1991, for Russian leaders
have traditionally been based on
US models. The factory, founded
in the 1930s, was originally called
Zavod Imjeni Stalina, but the
name was changed after the Soviet
leader's death in 1953 to Zavod
Imjeni Lihacheva. Lihacheva was
the director of the plant. This Zil-3
would have been in its heyday
during the early years following
the overthrow of Nikita Krushchev
by Leonid Brezhnev in 1964. The
chrome-laden car was powered by
an heroic, if not exactly proletarian,
200hp, six-litre V8. It could move.

81
1958 BMW 501

Leather-jacketed Munich
policeman with mighty 3.2-litre V8
501 patrol car. These voluptuous
cars were a mainstay of BMW car
production from 1951 to 1964.

79

82

83

82
1936 LANCIA

The defeated Ethiopian emperor, Haile Selassie (1892–1975), being paraded through Addis Ababa by Mussolini's men in 1936. The Italians used gas dropped by aircraft to crush the Ethiopian army. The Italians were, in turn, deposed by a British army composed largely of Indian soldiers in 1941. Haile Selassie, who claimed to be a direct descendant of King Solomon and the Queen of Sheba, was reinstated, but deposed by Communists in 1974. He was murdered the following year. Rastafarians believe him to have been an incarnation of God. At least in this picture he is travelling in regal style.

83
1921 ALFA ROMEO TIPO RLS

Here is Benito Mussolini (1883–1945), a man constantly in a hurry, arriving at a holiday hotel at the wheel of his fast and furious Tipo RLS. The fascist leader was dictator of Italy from 1922 to 1943. His attempt to establish an Italian empire to rival the glories of ancient Rome and his allegiance with Adolf Hitler caused his downfall. Captured by Italian partisans in 1945, he was executed and his torso hung upside in public as a warning to would-be fascists and their sympathizers. It had been a very long road from that Italian hotel entrance and that glorious Alfa.

84
1936 VOLKSWAGEN BEETLE

The People's Car – initially the KdF ("strength through joy") wagen – was to have been sold to Nazi party members for 1000 Reichsmarks, or about £85. Some 80,000 hopefuls signed up for their Ferdinand-Porsche-designed, 100km/h, air-cooled, streamlined, autobahn cruisers, but Hitler decided to invade Poland, ignite the Second World War and, ultimately, bring destruction on his own people. They had to wait some while before they could save up again for new VW Beetles. Here, in happier days, is Reichmarshall Hermann Göring being shown the underside of a new VW cabriolet by some strong Aryan übermenschen.

85
1935 ZIS

Iosif Vissarionovich Dzhugashvili, 1879–1953, (aka Stalin, Man of Steel) ran the Soviet Union with a rod of iron more or less from Lenin's death in 1924 to his own, from a stroke, in 1953. In the meantime, he may have seen the Soviet Union win its heroic victory over Nazi Germany, but he also killed millions of his countrymen in savage purges and wilful starvations. Like all dictators, he was fond of his cars. Here he is inspecting the first Zis-101 limousines inside the Kremlin on April 29, 1936. He is flanked, on his left, by I A Lihachov, director of Zis, and G K Ordjonikidze, minister of heavy industry, and, on his right, by V M Molotov (foreign secretary) and A I Mikoyan (trade secretary). The Zis was powered by a 90hp 6766cc straight-eight. Its top speed was 115km/h.

84

85

86

87

88

86 + 87 + 88
1930s MERCEDES-BENZ 540K
AND GROSSER MERCEDES
Adolf Hitler (1889–1945), *Time* magazine's Man of the Year, 1938, was devoted to Mercedes-Benz. He made the famous car company all but synonymous with his Nazi regime. He took a great interest in its cars, their design and engineering. Whenever, as in these three pictures, he was seen on public parade, it was in an open-top Mercedes. The cars were hugely powerful, all conquering, designed to last, all things that the Nazi regime was meant to be but thankfully wasn't. Designed to last 1,000 years, the Third Reich fell 988 years short of its target. The cars in these historic pictures have generally lasted much longer. The 770K Grosser Mercedes was prized by dictators and dodgy rulers worldwide. The Japanese emperor Hirohito ordered just the seven, while others were owned by General Franco of Spain, King Boris of Bulgaria and King Zog of Albania.

89
1936 MERCEDES-BENZ 540K
Adolf Hitler almost at the height of his power. This would continue to grow, like the output of the straight-eight motors of his Mercedes-Benz parade and touring cars, until Operation Barbarossa, the 1941 invasion of the Soviet Union. Hitler owned Mercedes-Benz cars from 1923, at the time of his failed coup in Munich, until his death.

89

90

**1942 VW TYPE-166
SCHWIMMWAGEN**
A parade of Porsche-designed
four-wheel-drive amphibians based
on the Kubelwagen, a military
adaptation of the Volkswagen.
The 166 was a popular troop carrier
and capable of 80km/h, but was
less popular in the water, where its
speed was no more than 10km/h,
and it was vulnerable to damage:
a single .303 bullet could sink it.
Some 15,000 Schwimmwagens
were built.

91

1953 VW BEETLE
Lined up on parade outside
Brunswick, these post-war Beetles
still have the look of SS guards on
parade at a Nazi rally. They were
to take the automotive world by
storm, and are still being made
today in Mexico.

92

92
1961 LINCOLN CONTINENTAL
A lovely day now the sun has broken through in Dallas, Texas on November 22, 1963. Moments later, president John F Kennedy would be gunned down by Lee Harvey Oswald. Stylish President, stylish first lady, stylish car: sensational and sad day. Ever since, US Presidents have ridden in vast armoured motorcades, taking no chances.

93
1961 LINCOLN CONTINENTAL
President John F Kennedy slumps over in the back of the open-topped car after being hit by Oswald's bullet. One of the iconic images of the twentieth century.

94

**94
MARTIN LUTHER KING'S 1965
CHEVROLET CHEVY II**
"I have a dream that my four
children will one day live in a
nation where they will not be
judged by the colour of their
skin but by the content of their
character." This is Dr Martin Luther
King (1929–68), Baptist pastor and
civil rights champion with his son
Martin Luther III, aged seven,
walking up to their house in
Georgia, Atlanta after church.
Dr King drove a modest car but
also drove an ambitious campaign
for human rights in the United
States. He was shot dead on the
steps of the Lorraine Hotel,
Memphis, Tennessee on April 4,
1968 by James Earl Ray.

95
1953 DAIMLER EMPRESS
The royal family is said to have
stopped using Daimlers in 1950,
but here is the young Queen
Elizabeth, with Prince Charles and
Princess Anne in tow, at the wheel
of what is surely a Hooper-bodied
Daimler Empress, probably on a
DE24 chassis. Whatever the truth,
the Queen looks happy to be
driving it. The Queen is a blood
relative of the former kaisers at the
time of the founding of the Daimler
car company in Germany; the
British Daimler company is related
only by association to what since
became the Daimler-Benz empire.
Frederick Richard Simms, an
Englishman, met Gottlieb Daimler
in 1880 and, later, created a
subsidiary of sorts back home.
In practice, the two companies
were entirely separate.

96
1958 LAND ROVER SERIES 1
HM Queen Elizabeth and HRH the
Duke of Edinburgh on board HMS
Albion in a Land Rover in 1959.
The Land Rover, based on the
wartime American Willys Jeep,
was only meant to be an Austerity-
era stop-gap model to be sold in
the colonies. Instead, it became
a national favourite, beloved of
farmers and the Queen. HMS
Albion was launched in 1947
and completed in 1954. Weighing
20,000 tons unladen, and powered
by 78,000hp Parson's steam
turbines, she could cruise at
20 knots for 6,000 miles non-stop.
She saw action in Suez, Aden and
Indonesia, was converted to a
helicopter carrier at the time of the
Queen's visit and was broken up in
1973. Land Rovers, including many
Series 1s, are still very much with
us. The Queen and the Duke of
Edinburgh, too.

96

97

98

1954 LAND ROVER SERIES 1
Here is Winston Churchill
(1874–1965) with his trademark
Cuban cigar and his favourite
Land Rover. The legendary wartime
leader was Prime Minister for a
second time (1951–55) when he
took delivery of his Land Rover. The
company had sold a record number
of cars in 1954, but Churchill's
support was to boost sales further.
The Land Rover certainly displayed
the "bulldog" characteristics that
had so endeared Churchill to the
nation as a wartime leader.

98
1943 WILLYS JEEP
The legendary General Purpose –
GP, and so "Jeep" – from Willys,
one of the all-time great cars. It did
much to help British, American and
Commonwealth troops during the
European campaigns of the Second
World War. Here Field Marshall
Montgomery, commander of the
Eighth Army that defeated Field
Marshall Rommel in the north
African desert, is chauffeured by
his regular driver J Burford. They
don't appear to be having much fun.

99
1943 WILLYS JEEP
President Franklin Delano
Roosevelt greets US troops
in Morocco in January 1943.
Everybody got to ride in a Jeep,
from a private to the President.

101

102

100
1967 WILLYS JEEP
"I love the smell of napalm in the morning"… US troops attempt to "completely level the Vietcong stronghold of Ben Suc" by torching the place. More than two million Vietnamese civilians died during the Vietnam War, along with some 58,000 US soldiers.

101
2003 LAND ROVER
Soldiers of the heavy machine gun platoon of the 1st battalion Irish Battle Group checking out a burning oil well during the US-UK invasion of Iraq, March 2003.

102
1991 AM GENERAL HUMMER
These vast off-road vehicles, seen here lining up on patrol in Saudi Arabia before heading to Iraq, were designed, from 1979, for the US army. Prototypes of the HMMWV (High Mobility Multipurpose Wheeled Vehicle), or Humvee or Hummer, were tested in 1982. The giant vehicle went into volume production in 1985. A civilian model followed after the publicity gained in the Gulf War in 1992. It became a cool "gangsta rappa" style accessory. Some accessory, and, to be honest, not much fun to drive even on the meanest city street. It comes into own well off the road, and, mostly, on the battlefield.

1955 BMW ISETTA 300
Cyclist about to overtake a Ford
Transit-based ambulance held up
on an English country lane by a
delightful example of *das rollende
ei*, BMW's "rolling egg" bubble car.
Not much fun at over 30mph, these
German-built Isettas – the original
cars were designed and built by
Isa, the Italian motorcycle
manufacturer – can beat 50mph,
but you would have to be brave to
aim for such giddy heights. Built
under licence from 1955 to 1964,
160,000 examples of the 300 were
made in Germany. Nearly all are
four-wheelers, although the
close-set rear pair means that
they are routinely mistaken for
three-wheelers. Engines are
either a 247cc or, more normally,
13hp 298cc single-cylinder BMW
motorcycle unit. Like all micro cars,
sales were hit hard by the arrival
of the BMC Mini in 1959.

106
1955 ISETTA MOTOCOUPE
How to travel in bubble car in
style. Employ a chauffeur. Dress
well. Wave from the sunroof while
pretending to be Princess Margaret
having a laugh. Do not exceed
30mph if you want your hair-do,
earrings or sanity to stay in place,
or one piece.

107
1955 BMW ISETTA
Let's do lunch! Smart lunching
ladies get aboard a 247cc Isetta
at the car's launch at the 1955
Earl's Court Motor Show.

106

107

108

109

108
1957 DKW JUNIOR
DKW went on to become Audi and the rest is a very successful history. This little American-style two-door coupe is the prototype DKW Junior, a twin-cylinder 660cc two-stroke mini car. Well engineered, although inevitably a little smoky, it went on to sell 118,968 examples.

109
1959 OPPERMAN STIRLING FAMILY SPEED SALOON
Designed by Lawrie Bond of Bond Minicars, the Stirling was a rather smart-looking two-door glass-fibre coupe that looked much like NSU's little Bertone-designed Sport Prinz. It could seat two adults and two children and, with a 424cc Excelsior two-stroke twin, could scurry up to a claimed 70mph. But it cost £541 7s, which meant it faced direct competition from the new Mini. Only two were built; one survives.

110
1959 NSU PRINZ 30
Who does he think he is? Stirling Moss… driving a German mini car. Moss, the great British racing driver, has always been fond of micro cars and motor scooters, the automotive opposite of the furiously fast racing cars he has piloted for more than 50 years. Here he is with a 1959 NSU Prinz sporting his own, personalized numberplate. The car had a 598cc 20hp twin. It would win no races.

111
1936 FIAT 500
No joke at all. This is a British-registered model with a sunroof in the rain at a Welsh rally in 1937. The 500, or "Topolino" ("Little Mouse", after Walt Disney's Mickey Mouse), was a superb little car, engineered by the motoring giant Fiat to standards that most of the independent post-war mini car makers were quite unable to match. The car was engineered by the brilliant Dante Giacosa during 1933–34 (he was just 28 years old when commissioned to undertake the project) and styled in-house by Fiat's Rudolfo Schaffer. The result is a very fine car. The engine is a 569cc in-line ohc watercooled unit with two valves per cylinder. The car features hydraulic brakes, 12-volt electrics, independent front suspension and a top speed of 85km/h. It handles well and rides like a much bigger car.

110

112

112
1957 FIAT 500
Twenty-one years later (see previous page), and the 50-year-old Giacosa produced a second mini triumph, the much-loved "Nouva 500" or "Cinquecento". It looked good in every setting, from the ducal square here in Turin to cobbled streets in every hill town you can think of. Approximately 3,678,000 were built in a number of guises, including an estate version, a beach "buggy" and a Topolino-lookalike that was also just like the illustrations for Noddy's car in Enid Blyton's children's stories. This time the car's engine was air-cooled – an enthusiastic 479cc twin – and mounted behind the tiny, four-seat cabin. The car could top 85km/h happily, and all day. Thousands roam the streets of Italian cities today.

113
1972 CLOCKWORK ORANGE
Pipped at the post… the Outspan orange advertising car squeezes to a halt at a zebra crossing in London. This funny car was based on the floorpan and running gear of a BMC Mini. Its job was to advertise South African oranges at a time when South Africa's policy of apartheid had made it one of the world's least liked regimes. The car survives in the National Motor Museum at Beaulieu, Hampshire.

114
1955 MESSERSCHMITT KR200
Like an Me-109 cockpit in search
of wings, the glorious KR was a
fine, fast two-seater. Here one
buzzes through Piccadilly Circus
trying to outdrag a quad of
handsome FX3 taxis, a Standard
Vanguard and a Morris Oxford. The
buses appear to be on strike,
so perhaps this is a scene from 1958
when the red buses disappeared
for weeks on end. The KR200 was
capable of 100km/h courtesy of
a 191cc Fichter and Sachs 10hp
single-cylinder, two-stroke engine.

115
1955 MESSERSCHMITT KR200
Carefree and not out to impress
anyone, a young chap whizzes along
in a single-seat, soft-top prototype.

116
1954 TYPE-C BOND MINICAR
Oh brave new world that hath such people in it… Ration books have just ended, so this happy family have decided to celebrate with a Bond Minicar. Stuff safety belts and all that palaver, they're motoring in true micro car style.

117
1960 NOBEL 200
Foxy lady seeks Noble. Noble, not Nobel. Aagh!

118
1967 HONDA N360
A thoroughly engineered Japanese rival for the well-established British Mini, the front-wheel-drive Honda N360 was neatly designed and drove well, with power – 31bhp, just 3bhp less than an 850 Mini – from a free-revving and jewel-like 354cc ohc twin. A larger 598cc was available from 1968, encouraging some export sales. But this was little more than an Oriental curiosity in the West at the time.

117

118

119
1983 SUZUKI CV
A 49cc retro-style mini show car by
the motorcycle giant.

120
1967 SUZUKI SHOW CAR
Things must have been getting
desperate. Mine's a Mini.

121
1957 GLAS T700
Hans Glas made his name with
his popular Goggomobil micro car,
but for those on their way up to
something a little bigger and more
like a real car, what about this
charming, two-tone American-style
sedan of 1957? The Fräulein in polka
dots is listening out for the 688cc
engine. Is it at the front or the back?
That would be telling, says Fritz.
Now kindly get off my bonnet; I can't
see where I'm going. This pretty car
was in production until 1965.

119

120

121

122
1967 MINI
How many 1960s fashion victims
can you fit in a Mini? Who knows,
man, I wasn't there. Fourteen is
the correct answer, in 1966, if
you must know.

123
1966 MINI COOPER S
Cooper S Minis won the tough,
long-distance Monte Carlo in
1964 and again in 1965. When
Timo Hakinen won again – seen
here battling through the snow
in "GRX 555D" – the French
authorities declared the win null
and void. The Mini had broken the
rules. How? It had the wrong sort
of headlamp bulbs, said the absurd,
and xenophobic, officials. It was
sweet revenge when a Cooper S
won again in 1967. The Cooper S
was a formidable car.

124
2002 MINI COOPER S
The new Mini is a chunky car
designed for the brawny streets of
US cities, such as Times Square in
the driving rain. It has been a big
success in New York. Except in
terms of its retro-aesthetic and
general layout, it is a very different
car from its sparky, if often poorly
built, predecessor. Although built
in England, the new Mini has been
engineered with considerable
BMW input and know-how.

122

123

124

1965 MORRIS MINI MINOR
The Mini was truly a classless and go-anywhere car, although blue-collar workers tended to prefer bigger, more conventional and more American-style Fords. To cover all class and age profiles, early Minis were badged Morris, Austin, Wolseley and Riley. The last two were meant to appeal to older, more conservative generations. Winsome and all but twee, they hold great appeal to Japanese collectors today, but very few are seen on British roads; many not so common, nor so garden, basic Minis are.

MINI CARS

CARS AND ARCHITECTURE

126

126
FORD MOTOR COMPANY MODEL-T
FACTORY, DETROIT, MICHIGAN
Today, most of the early Detroit
automobile factories are
abandoned ruins. This is Ford's
Model-T factory at the height of
the car's fame and sales success.
The photograph captures some, at
least, of the 50,000 employees who
laboured on the assembly lines
founded here in 1913. Henry Ford's
greatest architectural asset was
Albert Kahn. Born in Westphalia,
Germany, Kahn was to build more
than 600 factories, 521 of them
for Stalin in the Soviet Union.
The architect of the assembly line,
he created daunting, if seemingly
effortless, buildings stripped
almost of all decoration. These
captured the imagination of
writers, film directors and modern
European architects including
Le Corbusier. They were powerful
and unforgettable symbols of sheer
industrial might. The car, and,
above all, Ford, played a key role
in their development worldwide.

127
FORD ROTUNDA,
DEARBORN, MICHIGAN
Albert Speer, eat your heart out.
Designed by Albert Kahn for the
1933 Chicago World's Fair, this
dramatic exhibition pavilion was
deconstructed and shipped to
Ford's River Rouge Dearborn
factory in 1936. It was used to show
new cars, as here, for corporate
events and parties and for Ford's
children's Christmas season each
year until it burned down in 1962.
At one time the Rotunda was the
fifth most popular tourist attraction
in the United States.

FIAT LINGOTTO
FACTORY, TURIN

Speeding into space. Fiat test
drivers race around the great
roof of the magnificent five-storey
concrete factory that Giacomo
Matte-Trucco designed for Fiat
in the early 1920s. This scene
dates from 1929. The factory was
self-consciously modelled on Albert
Kahn's work for Ford in Detroit.
Le Corbusier was deeply impressed
by this machine age masterpiece;
he went so far as to describe it as
"a guideline for town planning".
Imagine anyone saying this in the
age of the Congestion Charge. The
factory no longer makes cars; it has
been converted by the Genoese
architect Renzo Piano, who once
designed a prototype car for Fiat in
the mid-1980s, into performance,
exhibition and meeting spaces. The
Lingotto factory retains its place in
the heart of industrial Turin.

129
AMERICAN SUBURBIA, 1952
In giving us freedom, the car also
gave us the ever expanding city.
So much so that, as early as the
mid-twentieth century, suburbia
has blossomed across – or blighted,
depending upon your point of
view – vast tracts of Britain and
the United States. Perhaps this
mattered less in the US, where
land, petrol and cars were all cheap
compared to little, precious and
costly Britain. With the car came
the garage, wider streets and the
decline of public transport. In
terms of urban planning and
architectural design, the car
gives and the car takes away.

130
ROUTE 4, ENGLEWOOD,
NEW JERSEY, 1935
As Fritz Todt engineered his
magnificent autobahns in
Germany, so the US federal
government pioneered its
seemingly boundless freeways.
The car scythed its way
unhindered through landscapes
worn and virgin. Here in New
Jersey, attempts were made to
civilize the new roads with smartly
uniform street lamps, generous
tree-planting and pedestrian
walkways. The scene seems less
innocent today, cars grinding
along nose to tail. Back in the
1930s, these roads seemed heroic;
nothing quite like them had been
built since the Romans.

129

131

132

131
SPAGHETTI JUNCTION, BIRMINGHAM, ENGLAND

There is a website called "How to Avoid Spaghetti Junction". This complex weave of concrete carriageways was never meant to be a nightmare. Designed by Owen Williams, engineer of Britain's first inter-city motorway, the M1, the US-style junction was meant to free traffic and not to twist it into a grid-locked tangle. There are times when this 1960s megastructure is quiet, but it lost its "white heat of technology" innocence years ago. Note how the heroic structure of the road junction contrasts with the dinky suburban housing estate alongside – a very English scene.

132
SEATTLE, 2000

Here, at the start of the twenty-first century, is the American city and its intimate relationship with the road and thus the car. Few developed countries are so dependent or quite so in love with the car. The scale of such roads defies common sense. Cars are fine in their place, but let's have some railways for heaven's sake. The US used to have some of the world's best long-distance trains. These were killed off by the end of the 1950s by cars rumbling along optimistic freeways.

133

133
DRIVE-IN MOVIE THEATRE,
COPENHAGEN, 1961
There are something like 550 cars
parked here on the opening night
of Scandinavia's first drive-in
movie theatre. How many can you
identify? The theatre might look
like a quarry to you and me, but
this was glamorous stuff in 1961,
adopted from the US.

134
DRIVE-IN MOVIE THEATRE,
LOS ANGELES, c 1945
This is the original, or one of them:
an LA drive-in when Bogart and
Bergman were among the stars of
this very big screen. Note the
loudspeakers blaring into the cars.
The drive-thru burger restaurant,
bank and whatever else were to
follow soon enough.

134

US CAR PARK, c 1940

A sea of veteran Americana. It was
a delight for car enthusiasts, but a
nightmare for many people as the
car began to eat up land hungrily
from the 1930s. By the way, who
says that cars all look the same
today and didn't then?

CARS AND ARCHITECTURE

136
MULTI-STOREY CAR PARK,
BRISTOL, 1960
Parking spaces in British cities were always going to be a problem; as the number of cars sold rocketed during the consumer boom of the late 1950s, so local authorities began investing in multi-storey car parks such as this 550-space concrete behemoth. Although often despised, these were necessary structures if the car was to be king, queen and all princes in our city centres. The delightful thing here is the contrast between the spindly looking cars – a Ford Anglia and a Standard Vanguard estate – and the Space Age heroics of the architect-designed garage they creep in and out of. The men in white coats have long gone.

137
AUTOMATIC CAR PARK,
SOUTHWARK, LONDON, c 1961
This was one way of cramming 464 parked cars into a restricted space: raise and slide them into position on steel racks. This one has just opened near London Bridge, shortly before it was sold off to an American buyer and replaced by a new one. The period cars include a Riley 1.5, Austin A40, Hillman Minx, Ford Consul Mk2, Jaguar Mk2 and Vauxhall Victor.

138

138
1955 CITROEN DS19
Much like the exquisite sixteenth
century French tapestry depicting
the Unicorn in Captivity, on show
in the Cloisters museum, New York,
Flaminio Bertoni's superb Citroën
DS sits captive in a circular
compound fenced off from the
prosaic cars around it. This was the
Paris motor show, 1955. By the end
of the first day, Citroën had taken
12,000 orders for the car, proof
that the public is not always as
old-fashioned as it is often made
out to be. Bertoni (1903–64) had
designed the Citroën Traction
Avant as well as its 2CV. The DS –
deese, or goddess – was his third
masterpiece. Its qualities are as
much architectural as they are
mechanical; it inspired a new
generation of architects, designers
and even philosophers. "I think that
cars today," wrote Roland Barthes,
"are almost the exact equivalent
of the great Gothic cathedrals:
I mean the supreme creation of
an era, conceived with passion by
unknown artists, and consumed in
image if not in usage by a whole
population which appropriates
them as a purely magical object."

139
**SHOPPING MALL, SAINT
LAURENT, FRANCE, 1970**
No car, no shopping mall. The
two have developed hand in hand.
Here, in a wonderfully bland new
French mall, the cars have come
inside. Why not? They belong here
as much as "Byron", "Singer" and
"Timwear". The cars on show are
the new, air-cooled Citroën GS
mixing it with the last generation of
the epoch-making Citroën DS and
the bouncy little Ami.

140

141

140
MONT BLANC TUNNEL,
FRENCH-ITALIAN ALPS, 1965
Not even the Alps were a challenge
for the car. Hannibal had crossed
them with elephants in 218BC,
but, from July 16, 1965 families in
sturdy Peugeot 404s like this one
could drive straight through them.
At 11.6km, the tunnel was the
longest of its kind in the world. It
was closed for three years after a
devastating fire caused death and
much damage on March 24, 1999.

141
OAKLAND BAY BRIDGE,
SAN FRANCISCO, 1936
Road bridges are an art never quite
perfected, but always stirring and
often magnificent. This great steel
suspension bridge over Oakland
Bay was opened by President
Roosevelt on November 12, 1936.
The President has only just cut
the ribbon here as a stream of
cars rumbles over the brave new
$77.6 million structure. It was
considered one of the new wonders
of the world at the time.

142
UNDERPASS, MANHATTAN c 1960
By the 1960s, cars were passing
over, under, below, between and
beside the streets of our cities.
Like ants on the march, nothing, it
seemed, could stop them. Here cars
plunge down from New York's city
district. City Hall is the backdrop
along with all-American billboards
for Coca-Cola and Pall Mall
cigarettes, long before the Surgeon-
General had determined that they
were bad for your health. Before
seat belts and emission tests, too.

142

143

144

145

SIMON'S DRIVE-IN COFFEE
SHOP, LOS ANGELES, 1951
This drive-in was in Hollywood.
It took its design cue from neon-lit
movie theatres. You could either sit
inside, like models from an Edward
Hopper painting, or be served by
a smartly uniformed waitress
without moving your ever bigger
butt from behind the wheel.

144
GAS STATION, WENDOVER,
UTAH, c 1945
This shot captures the notional
romance of long-distance driving,
US-style. The cinematic gas
station offers not just fuel for the
car, but fuel for the inner man,
too, and "cabins" to rest up in for
the night. It has its own special,
low-rent glamour.

145
GAS STATION, MINNEAPOLIS,
MINNESOTA, 1937
The speed of the car encouraged
forms of architecture that could be
seen and identified from a distance,
and by night. This spectacular
1930s gas station was built almost
entirely in glass bricks so that it
shone like a single giant lamp at
night. A delightful conceit.

PETROL STATION, BLASHFORD, HAMPSHIRE, 1930

That'll be ye olde petrol station, sir. Odd of you to be driving a foreign car, sir. What is it? A Renault, you say… A venerable thatched petrol station complete with leaded-light windows dating, it seems, from the sixteenth century. Or, how to motor the English way even when driving a car built by Johnny French. Long gone, sadly.

147

GULF LIGHTHOUSE SERVICE STATION, MIAMI BEACH, FLORIDA, 1937

Lovely period artwork for this new, nautical-style service station inspired clearly by the speed and shape of cars, as well as its setting by the ocean. It offers not just gas, air and water for the car, but also a hotel with restaurant and cocktail bar. Saves drinking and driving then; not that many drivers seemed to think this was a problem in the 1930s.

148

PONTIAC SERVICE STATION, MEXICO CITY, 1942

Great combination of Mexican hacienda-style architecture and unconstrained neon advertising hoarding. The car was very much king at this time; no apologies need to be made for it, neither in the amount of fuel it used nor in the way buildings designed to serve it affected the look and feel of city streets.

146

147

148

CARS AND ADVERTISING

One of my favourite advertisements here is for Bugatti (page 164). It shows a very stylish young lady about to drive off in her black and yellow Type 57, one of the finest cars ever built. There are no words. Correction. There is just the one. In the bottom right-hand corner is the legend "Bugatti", a badge of unqualified excellence. It seems a wonder that Bugatti bothered to advertise at all. Word of mouth, or simply the sight of those matchless cars, or the sound of their exhausts – tearing calico; it's always "tearing calico" with a Bugatti exhaust – would be enough, you would have thought, to have got the cheque books out in the 1920s and 1930s.

The point here is that Bugatti needed no fine words to butter mechanical parsnips. Its cars were meat and vegetables, pudding, fine wines, champagne and brandy, too. Lesser marques have needed to sell their cars hard, and often, although not always, there is a rule of thumb that works: the worse the car, the fancier the advert needed to sell it.

The unintended humour of the advert for the Ford Edsel on page 167 is delightful. "They'll know you've arrived when you drive up in an Edsel." They certainly will. They will also run a mile or crack up laughing. The poor old Edsel – not such a bad car, really – was one of the biggest flops in motoring history. Subject of an unprecedented $250 million advertising campaign, the car was launched just as the US economy was taking a nose-dive. No one, not even most of Ford's management, liked the name (it belonged to Henry Ford's son) and many people actively disliked the car's trademark "horse-collar" grille. Whatever the reasons not to buy, Ford sold just 100,847 Edsels – again, not that bad – during its production run between 1957 and 1960, with a further 7,431 sold in Canada. It had banked on selling 200,000 in 1957 alone.

The advertising slogan for the Mk C Bond Minicar is equally, if less disastrously, funny. "You too ought to own a Bond Minicar," it says. Note the "ought". Perhaps you *ought* to, but one look at the curious cartoon-style car says you just might not want to own one.

Real humour is still rare in car advertising. Volkswagen, or its ad agency, DD&B (Doyle Dane Bernbach, founded in 1948), used it particularly well when it needed to fend off impending competition from the US auto industry big guns, who had the Beetle very much in their sights in 1959. The first run of press ads were disarmingly simple. Not only were there no girls, stables or country houses in the background, there was no background whatsoever. Just crisp, clean black and white photographs of the car. Designed and copywritten by Helmut Krone and Julian Koening, the first showed a tiny VW and read "Think Small". This, of course, was when most of America was thinking BIG. Big houses, big refrigerators, big TVs, big cars.

A second series of ads for the Beetle in 1960 included the brilliant "Lemon" ad. That's what it said under another undoctored photo of the Beetle. Lemon, because this is what the car might appear to be to drivers of huge, swanky Yankee gas-guzzlers of the time.

Well, how would you sell the Beetle, an air-cooled, 100km/h people's car developed in Nazi Germany to be sold for 100 Reichmarks (about £85 or $350) to the party faithful? Yet, the advertising strategy worked. Americans took the "Bug" to their auto-hearts, as they did its sporting sibling, the VW Karmann-Ghia. This pretty, but distinctly sluggish, soft-top was marketed in the States as "the world's least powerful sports car". These campaigns worked well. Sales of all cars imported to the US fell considerably between 1959 and 1963, but those of Volkswagens rose significantly.

Significant, too, is the fact that DD&B had never worked for the motor industry before. Free of the industry's tired clichés, sexism and conservatism, the agency was able to come up with something fresh, and very effective. The ads were later translated to TV. One of the most memorable shows a Beetle battling through a snowstorm. The voiceover says ,"Did you ever wonder how the man who drives the snowplough gets to the snowplough?"

Audi's enjoyable *Vorsprung durch technik* (progress through technology) campaign, dating from 1984, was in much the same tradition. It played up the way that the world sees German engineers, scientists and technicians as eccentric yet meticulous and even zealous types with clipboards and white coats. By this time, the marque was a familiar one in Britain and the US. Not long before, Audi ran a campaign, "Owdy!", to ensure that potential buyers could actually pronounce the name of the cars. Interestingly, Braun UK decided that it had all been too much to expect Brits to pronounce foreign names, and although Braun is the same as Brown, in sound and meaning, the British arm of the company decided to call itself "Brawn".

Our unintentionally funny advertising includes one of the brochures kept on my bookshelves. This one is for a finless MkV Sunbeam Alpine. I like the words "powerful" and "high performance", the blonde dolly so impressed by the hunk holding the keys to the car, the no-nonsense Bell helicopter and press cameraman in the background. In truth – I know because I once owned one – the Sunbeam, for all its gentle, cheery charms, is a bit of a lemon. It is not powerful, its performance is limited and, truth be told, it is not really a sports car.

Nor, I suppose, was the much-loved MGB, or at least not in its flabby, later days when its pretty mouth was gagged with rubber and its suspension was raised too high to take corners seriously. What could a British advertising agency in the flared and sideburned 1970s do with it? Describe it as a "mistress" while referring to its "beautiful body… a joy to handle". This was not the worst of these Carry On-meets-Penthouse-style ads. Try the 1971 ad for the Mini automatic on page 175.

Still cars and lagery, laddish ads seem destined, like Mrs Thatcher, and her legacy, to go on and on. At least Kylie Minogue, a Forces' sweetheart of our times, looks sweet and bright rather than the car industry's usual dumb and pouting stretched across the bonnet of a soft-top Ford StreetKa. Not quite Bugatti, of course, but a long(ish) way from the sexist excesses of the 1960s and 1970s.

151

151

1935 BUGATTI TYPE 57C

This is a perfect, hand-tinted shot from a 1935 Bugatti brochure. It needs few words, and in fact there is only one – the neatly understated name of the fabulous marque. The smart young lady heading happily for the driving seat is lucky indeed. This particular model, designed largely by Jean Bugatti, short-lived son of Ettore Bugatti, the marque's founder, is just one of three Type 57Cs bodied by Atalante with a sunroof that slides down like a roll-top desk. Altogether, just 630 3.3-litre Type 57s – about 100 of them supercharged and good for 120mph – were built between 1934 and 1939. Bugatti spelt brilliance. There have been few finer cars before, then, or since.

152

1938 NASH AMBASSADOR

Nash, one of America's most successful independent car manufacturers at the time, bought Kelvinator, the refrigeration company, in 1938. This might explain Nash's pioneering development of air-conditioning in cars. The "Weather Eye conditioned air system" advertised here for the '38 Nash wasn't air-conditioning as we know it, but it was an excellent advance on the vast majority of contemporary cars worldwide that suffered badly from condensation in anything other than fine weather. It's freezing outside as the fur-wrapped doorman testifies, but it's so comfortable inside the big, eight-cylinder Nash that this elegant dame can leave her mink stole on the back of the plush seat. This advert would have had a big impact in the 1930s.

NO MORE FROZEN RIDES...OPEN WINDOWS FOR WINTER VENTILATION... CHILLING DRAFTS...FOGGED WINDOWS...DUSTY, GRIMY TRIPS...INSECTS...SMOKY AIR...OR STUFFY CARS ...the World's First Car with a "Conditioned-Air System" for winter driving is here! Always 70° comfort in zero weather. A revolutionary feature—exclusive with Nash!

WAY BELOW ZERO *And No Wrap!*

152

"Blazin[...]
attacks[...]
Jeeps, [...]
Chinese[...]
inspired[...]
vital po[...]
Chiang[...]
truly in[...]
peddlin[...]
ad from[...]
with th[...]
car. It w[...]
finest w[...]
World V[...]
and ulti[...]
dozens[...]
continu[...]

157

1951 BOND MK B MINICAR

Gosh, mummy and daddy, look what I've found in the woods! Crikey, Susan, it's just what we've always wanted: a super Bond Minicar! Rather! This toy-like 197cc trike is advertised here, appropriately, in the pictorial style of that ever-so-English cartoon hero, Rupert Bear, and his adventures in Nutwood (and the *Daily Express* newspaper). The Bond had first appeared in 1949, but was very slow indeed. This model, a response to customers, boasted a bigger 197cc Villiers Mk 6E single-cylinder engine,

a top speed of 50mph and a fuel consumption of between 75 and 80mpg. The arrival of the BMC Mini in 1959 effectively put paid to British micro cars, although production of the Bond Minicar continued up to the 250cc, 60mph Mk G in 1966. About 26,500 Bond Minicars had been made, in Preston, Lancashire, over 15 years.

158

1957 AUSTIN A55 CAMBRIDGE

It is easy to imagine these solid English cars chugging down some warm and sunny A-road towards the summer beaches of Devon and

Cornwall… forever. These were modest cars with some pretension to transatlantic styling: just look at all that jazzy chrome, that daring two-tone paintwork. Built between 1957 and 1959 – it was replaced by crisper, Pinin-Farina-designed models – the A55 could top 75mph when hurried and accelerate to 60mph from start in 31.8 seconds. This is a pre-motorway age car in the setting it was very much designed for; the British economy had recently taken off after years in the doldrums and people were dreaming of life as a prolonged summer holiday.

153

AVEN[...]

B[...]
[...]
[...]
[...]

In China,[...]
this way, the[...]
and with sm[...]

No assign[...]
weather is s[...]

157

Announcing the arrival in this country of the famous

HEINKEL Cabin Cruiser

Sept. 1956

TRAVEL IN STYLE FOR A PENNY A MILE

exceedingly
FAST

very
MOBILE

extremely
ECONOMICAL

interior spacious and
COMFORTABLE

SOLE CONCESSIONNAIRES
For GREAT BRITAIN and THE BRITISH COMMONWEALTH

MESSERSCHMITT

MESSERSCHMITT KR 200
BEULAH HILL ENGINEERING COMPANY LIMITED
Telegrams : Cabinscoot, London   LONDON, S.E.19   Telephone: GIPsy Hill 4262 (6 lines)

160

VELAM

Isetta

161

1956 HEINKEL CABIN CRUISER
I say, is that Hermann Göring the lady is waving to? I mean, the plump chap at the wheel of the new German bubble car. Sorry, my little mistake. In fact, it's a jolly chap off with his family in his "exceedingly" fast, pear-drop-shaped car. The ad says the little car is "spacious and comfortable", although Mum's head and shoulder appear to be squished against the windscreen, or front door, or whatever you call it. This was the heyday of the European bubble car. It was not to last very long. Bet the family was pleased. The *kleine* Stuttgart *wunder* was built under licence in England, Argentina and Ireland until 1964.

160
1955 MESSERSCHMITT KR 200
A family of vampires tries to scare potential buyers from Great Britain and the Commonwealth away from the tiny, tandem-seat "Kabin Roller". Actually, the Messerschmitt was, in many ways, the best of the 1950s micro cars. It was imaginatively engineered, by Messerschmitt's Fritz Fend, well built, aerodynamically efficient, stable and fun to drive. Its 1940s Me109-style canopy was eyecatching and witty. Fend approached Willy Messerschmitt with the idea of making his earlier Flitzer mini car at the redundant aircraft works at Regensburg. Until 1956, Messerschmitt was banned from making aircraft. After discussions, the KR 200 emerged from the Messerschmitt factory. This was sold to Fend after 1956 when Messerschmitt returned to aircraft design. The KR 200's single-cylinder, fan-cooled, 191cc two-stroke engine will get it up to 60mph; steering, through an aircraft-style control column, is direct; and it will fit through gaps that a Harley-Davidson might refuse. The cars were built until 1964.

161
1957 VELAM ISETTA
A stylish Parisian lady goes to the fashion shops in her French-built Isetta. These bubble cars, nicely described by one enthusiast as a collision between a fridge, a motor scooter and an aeroplane, were first designed and made by Renzo Rivolta's Iso; Iso, a fridge manufacturer, turned to making scooters and cars in the 1950s. Then came the Isetta, which was made, under licence, in a number of countries including France. Only BMW bothered to develop the tiny four-wheeler, and this French version soon vanished from Paris boulevards, a fashion statement, here *aujourd'hui*, gone *demain*.

recapture true motoring pleasure with

Riley *One-Point-Five*

Powerful '1725' engine

HIGH PERFORMANCE **SUNBEAM** *Alpine*

162

1957 RILEY 1.5

Kangol driving cap, string-backed leather driving gloves, detailed road maps, an ignition key, and off we go, Riley-style, into the A- and B-roads of 1950s Britain. The Riley was really a badge-engineered Morris Minor. Riley, like many independent British car makers, had been swallowed up by this time by the mighty British Motor Corporation (BMC). Still, the 1.5 was remarkably sporting. With a twin-carb 1,489cc engine, slick gearchange and uprated suspension, it cut quite a dash on the road. It did well in races and rallies, too. By the time production ceased in 1965, it must have seemed upright, old-fashioned and rather quaint. I had one as a runabout for five years from 1987; it was the most reliable car that I have ever owned.

163

1965 SUNBEAM ALPINE MKV

This was the last of the five series of pretty, civilized sports cars built by Rootes to the designs of, mostly, Kenneth Howes and his assistant Roy Axe. Howes had been trained as a locomotive apprentice with the Great Western Railway, Swindon, before moving on to Raymond Loewy's industrial design studios in London and New York, and from there to Studebaker and Ford. He brought American flair and comfort to this smart little sports tourer. The MkV model, the fastest and most comfortable of all, lacked the exaggerated fins of its predecessors, but was still an eye-catching design. Production ceased in 1968. Cars fitted with Ford 289 cubic inch V8s were known as Tigers. They really did roar. And go. This period brochure shows a smart Kensington gal allowing herself to be impressed by the James Bond wannabe who has just stepped out from the pilot's seat of a Bell helicopter and is being snapped by a press cameraman. The Alpine was never really quite so glamorous. But its owners could always dream.

1963 FORD CORTINA MK1

Chaps and chapesses off to a West End black-tie do in an East End 1200cc Cortina from Dagenham. It seems a bit unlikely. The Cortina was never – except in Lotus-Cortina guise – going to have much appeal for toffs. It was a lightweight, simple, kit-of-parts composed of earlier Ford models, but built on a generous scale and quite lively out on the motorway age roads. Although looking every inch a product of Detroit, it was named after the stylish Italian winter resort Cortina di Ampezzo, where the popular 1956 Winter Olympics had been held. The rumour was that Ford's British chairman, Patrick Hennessey, had wanted to call the new

medium-sized saloon the "Caprino", but changed his mind when he learned this was Italian for "goat dung". The car was launched in September 1962. It sold very well indeed and, after its demise in 1965, it spawned three more generations of best-selling, good-value Cortinas.

165

1956 VW KARMANN-GHIA

Or the other way around, as in this German ad celebrating the car's intelligence and elegance for an elegant and intelligent audience, presumably, rather than for its power, which it most definitely lacked. This pretty, popular and long-lived car – the last were built in 1974 – had started life as a Ghia

show car for Chrysler. Chrysler wasn't interested. When VW approached Karmann for a sports car, the German coachbuilder turned to Ghia, which came up with the Chrysler design… Mated to a Beetle chassis and its 1,192cc air-cooled engine, the Karmann-Ghia was born. There were many lovely ads for this car; one American TV ad showed the VW racing towards a paper screen held up by two white-coated boffins. Will it, won't it? No. The car is stopped in its tracks by the screen. "Volkswagen Karmann-Ghia", said the tongue-in-cheek commentary, "the world's least powerful sports car". It worked. What the car did have, though, was catwalk rather than assembly line looks.

Intelligenz
gepaart mit
Eleganz

Ghia-Karmann kombiniert vernunft-gegebene technische Daten mit modischer Höchsteleganz, kombiniert die bekannte Strapazierfähigkeit und aussergewöhnliche Wirtschaftlichkeit des VW mit luxuriösem Fahrkomfort und einer meisterhaft gestalteten, äusserst schnittigen, repräsentativen Karosserie.

Ghia-Karmann: der VW im Galakleid!
Er vereinigt den Traum des kalkulierenden Automobilisten mit dem Luftschloss der verwöhnten Fahrerin… vereinigt sie zu Wirklichkeit und doppeltem Fahrgenuss!

Amag Schinznach-Bad

166
1963 FIAT 1500 SPIDER

Quite why this svelte lady is sporting scuba-diving equipment in this blatantly sexist ad for the pretty, open-top Fiat 1500 is anyone's guess. Might there be torrential rain along the Via Appia? Is the smug dork with the Fiat's keys (yes, you the 1960s bloke supposedly gawping at the ad and dreaming of fast Italian cars and even faster Italian ladies) likely to be unable to stop before plunging into the sea at Amalfi? Who knows.

167
1975 MGB GT

But is this a saloon car or a sports car? And if this ugly, rubber-nosed version of the once pretty MGB GT is a sports car, why run away with her rather than spend a weekend with the wife. All this is nonsense, of course. As is this sensationally dumb advert from MG in the dark days of British Leyland ownership. The MGB GT was a charming sports tourer – the MGB given a Pininfarina design makeover and metal roof – not quick, but characterful. It was bought by the sort of people who tended to keep them for years, which very few mistresses are.

168
1972 MG MIDGET

She probably would, actually. The 1275cc Midget was a sweet natured and fine handling little sports car that would be just the thing for buzzing along Devon lanes in search of a slap-up cream tea with Aunty Madge and the new vicar. Here it is, posed outside every Sloane Rangers' favourite emporium, the General Trading Company, caught in a tide of entertaining clothes and trying to look groovy in Day-Glo orange paint, striped fabrics and Rostyle wheels, despite its venerable engineering.

166

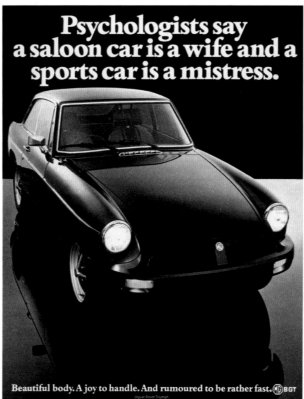

167

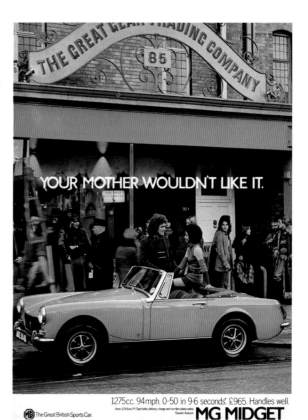

168

The Mini automatic. For simple driving.

This dizzy Goldie Hawn lookalike (one of the stars of NBC's hugely popular "Rowan and Martin's Laugh In" TV comedy, 1968–73) is doing her best to drive a Mini Clubman Automatic. Few cars could be easier, but at least she's trying. Gosh, what an amusing ad. This is the best the dreadful British Leyland, a corporation that did its level best to destroy the British car industry in the 1970s, could do. Dumb, funny only perhaps to leering salesmen in kipper ties, wide lapels and Jason King moustaches drinking lager-tops and smoking Players Number Six, this ad was enough to make anyone look abroad for their next car. Can you read the last paragraph? "It makes driving as effortless as sleeping. Sleeping, luv. You lie down, close your eyes and…" Those three dots would have meant a lot to the boys at British Leyland. Know what I mean, squire?

Optional automatic transmission available on all models except 850 and G.T. at £97.18.4. inc. p.t

The Mini automatic does one little thing more for you.

It changes gear without you changing gear. This little thing can make a world of difference in all kinds of driving conditions.

In congested traffic you don't fight a running battle with the gear stick. The gearbox fights its own battles.

When you're driving fast you keep both hands on the wheel all the time, which makes for a safer ride. And whenever you feel like a bit of fast armwork through the bends, you can switch from automatic to manual.

Then our automatic has some hidden benefits. You can't stall on the clutch because there's no clutch pedal to stall on.

You can't grind into the wrong gear because you don't change gear. In fact the Mini automatic is the closest thing you'll find to a built-in chauffeur.

It makes driving as effortless as sleeping. Sleeping, luv. You lie down close your eyes and…

Mini

Mini: greatest invention since the wheel.

1986 AUDI 80

A very funny advert for the new Audi 80 by the London agency BBH, who had created the German marque's famous "Vorsprung durch technik" campaign. Here, the ad pretends to explain what exactly the scientific sounding phrase means. The answer is an encyclopedia's worth of Germanic engineering gobbledy-gook, ending with the sort of difficult mathematical equation that would have had Einstein scratching his head. In tiny letters in English at the bottom of the ad, it says "To fully understand Vorsprung Durch Technik you need a fine grasp of German and the mind of a German engineer. However, you can experience it by driving the new Audi 80". Clever. Very clever indeed. By the way, it means "progress through technology". More or less.

171
2003 FORD STREETKA

The neat curves of this tiny roadster based on the fish-like Ford Ka were, or so Ford's advertising team thought, neatly mirrored by the even neater curves of tiny Australian pop minstrel Kylie Minogue. So here's the Vera Lynn, the Forces' sweetheart, of our times, disporting herself and her globally famous bottom, across the pert bonnet of the imaginatively priced, fashion-conscious Ford. This is cute in a knowing, post-modern, retro-chic way, but was Ford being serious? Maybe. Kylie launched a range of underwear in London in 2003 and it sold like Model-Ts. Could Kylie pull off the same trick for the Ford StreetKa? Probably not, because the car itself was not much to write home about. Ford should be so lucky.

170

171

DREAM CARS

172
1935 HUDSON CUSTOM EIGHT
Just what is he saying, and why is she smiling? Who knows? Whatever these two are up to, they've arrived in a very dashing Hudson. It's a lovely summer's day and there must surely be a handsome wicker hamper and a chilled bottle of champagne in the trunk of the semi-streamlined sedan. This is an enduring dream; the car as mechanical Cupid.

173
1945 RILEY RMA 1.5-LITRE
A very British, austerity era dream… The rakish, fabric-roofed, two-tone Riley is nowhere near as fast as it looks. With just 55hp under its dashing bonnet, this car will be pressed to beat 75mph. But it cuts a lovely dash, and the girls will soon be on their refined, twin-cam way from the airfield to scones and cream in some chintzy cheery Sussex tea shop, I'll be bound.

173

174
1936 MERCEDES-BENZ 540K CABRIOLET

The mighty 500/540K cabriolets were never really the Nazi monsters that they have been labelled. Designed by Hans Nibel, they were truly magnificent machines designed to cruise at very high speeds in their high fourth gears along Fritz Todt's new autobahns. But they were not just fast; they were sophisticated, too. The 112mph supercharged 540K featured power-assisted brakes and independent suspension, front and rear. Bodywork varied from the gross to the voluptuous. They remain completely in their element along sweeping autobahns, dream cars that have long outlived the Nazi nightmare.

175
1937 MERCEDES-BENZ 540K SPECIAL ROADSTER

Hermann Göring's favourite car. Even so, a truly beautiful mechanical Valkyrie, and almost a parody of the dream, open-topped roadster. That impossibly long bonnet, pert rump, sweeping running boards, chromed exhaust pipes, tiny windscreen and just the two, well-cushioned leather seats. And does it go? Exactly as it looks. And as it should with a 180hp, 5401cc supercharged straight eight. Just 26 of these three-ton Wagnerian supercars were built, with bodies by MB's own *karoserrie* in Sindelfingen. They cost 28,000 Reichsmarks (28 times the price of a Volkswagen) and 40 per cent more than the most expensive V16 Cadillac.

175

176
1934 CHRYSLER AIRFLOW
Here tradition means modernity
as a cluster of highly posed New
England huntsmen stop to take a
gander at this latest streamlined
wonder. A brave stylistic move by
Walter Chrysler, the Airflow was
the automotive equivalent of
William Van Alen's iconic Chrysler
Building scraping the sky in
mid-town Manhattan. Sadly, the
public found it hard to take to the
car's looks, especially its waterfall
grille. It also suffered more than its
fair share of teething problems.
And yet the Airflow, developed by
Carl Breer with advice from Orville
Wright, and with the aid of a new
wind tunnel at the Chrysler works,
led the way to the architecture of
the modern car. A flawed dream,
but one that was to change the way
cars looked worldwide.

177
1940 FORD V8 CONVERTIBLE
Okay, you couldn't afford a drop-
top V16 Cadillac; well, what about
this for just $849? With a sturdy
V8 engine under the hood and
snazzy looks, this 1940 Ford offered
cheap(ish) and glamorous motoring
to people like these in the period
advert, who wanted the good life
but had average incomes.

177

178
1945, BRANDENBURG GATE, BERLIN
The Nazis have gone – hoorah – but the Russians, British, French and Americans have yet to go away, and, meanwhile, the Martians appear to have landed and are pootling down Unter den Linden in their peculiar Earth Modules… The dreams of the impending Space Age were expanding in the minds of eccentric designers, who included Fritz Fend, the man responsible for these Flitzers.

179
1945 ZIS 110 LIMOUSINE
The Soviet proletariat could only dream. The mighty seven-seater Zis was never put on sale. It was reserved for the Communist Party elite. It was also, rather engagingly, a handsome rehash of the 1942 Packard Super Eight. One of these plutocratic capitalist cars had been presented to Stalin by President Roosevelt in 1942 as a goodwill gesture. Powered by a mighty 6005cc straight eight, the three-ton Zis could sweep up to 140km/h on Moscow's vast roads, passengers hidden behind plush velvet curtains and armour plate.

180
1959 PLYMOUTH SPORT FURY CONVERTIBLE
One way of spending Sunday afternoon with a long-necked lady or two. What on earth did the lady in the Chinese hat think of Bud's decision to take her for a spin in a zoo? How did they end up in the giraffe enclosure? Did the power brakes on the svelte new Sport Fury fail? Unlikely. These were cars were tough as well as chic. Powered by a 318 cubic inch, 230hp V8, they were also powerful beasts. Was this ad meant to prove that the '59 Plymouth was as elegant,

exotic and as long legged as a giraffe? Whatever, it evokes the idea of escapism on wide open freeways that, with the right car, might just take you anywhere.

181
1955 FORD THUNDERBIRD
American soldiers coming home from Europe between 1945 and 1955 brought many sports cars back with them. But where was the affordable all-American sports car? It remained a dream until the launch of two legendary rivals, the glass-fibre-bodied Chevrolet

Corvette in 1953 and the all-steel Ford Thunderbird two years later. The T-Bird offered American levels of comfort and even automatic transmission, but with real style and performance. It could top 115mph and cover the standing quarter mile in 17 seconds. Jaguar XKs were faster, but T-Birds were relaxed cruisers as well as pretty quick. Named after the New Mexican thunder god, and styled by Frank Hershey and William P Boyer, the Thunderbird was to become one of the enduring icons of American design.

188

1959 JAGUAR MK2

Set in an idyllic English Cotswold country house scene, here is the quintessence of English saloon car design in one of its natural habitats. The house is actually a bit of an upstart, a twentieth century take on an old Cotswold home, just as the dynamic Jaguar was a bit of an upstart, too. Not quite a Bentley, and a little uncouth when pushed hard. Never mind, Jaguar's William Lyons knew exactly how to realize grand motoring dreams for relatively little money. The 3.8-litre Mk2 was the fastest four-door saloon car in the world when launched in 1959: 125mph and acceleration from rest to 100mph in 25 seconds was very much a reality.

189

1968 LOTUS ELAN S4 AND LOTUS ELAN 2 + 2

Here is Colin Chapman (1928–82), one of the great British car designers, outside his home with two of his nimble sports cars. Chapman, a one-time RAF flying officer, played an enormous role in the development of Formula One racing. He also designed and built a range of very successful, hugely enjoyable lightweight sports cars, including this pair of short- and long-wheelbase Elans. Each Chapman Lotus was pared to its alloy bones. They remain thrilling to drive today, truly modern cars that played to Ludwig Mies van der Rohe's famous architectural maxim: less is more. Strange, then, that Chapman's house seems so very old-fashioned and unstylish – my dears, just look at those net curtains – but that's England for you. We dream of compromise in all things. And even the Elan was forced to live with a wood-veneered dashboard.

188

190

190

1963 ASTON MARTIN DB4

Styled by Touring of Milan, with a chassis by Harold Beach and powered by Tadek Marek's magnificent 3.7-litre, twin-overhead-cam straight six, this is one of the great cars. Nothing in excess. Simple fighter-style cabin. No wood. Little in the way of chrome. Lightweight body construction. 140mph. Launched to critical acclaim in 1958. Replaced by the *Goldfinger*-style DB5 in 1964. Only bettered by the faster, short-wheelbase DB4 GT.

191

1946 CISITALIA 202

The dream of a former footballer and amateur racing driver turned business magnate, Piero Dusio, the Cisitalia was styled by Pininfarina and Vignale and was one of the most stylishly modern cars of its time. It must have seemed a dream when first displayed to the public at the Italian Grand Prix in 1947. The car had a racing spaceframe chassis, and making liberal use of components from the workaday Fiat 1100, it was a perfectly practical proposition. Performance was lively from the 60hp 1089cc Fiat engine because the car was so light. Its forward-looking styling earned it a place in the New York Museum of Modern Art's permanent design collection.

192

1965 ASTON MARTIN DB5

With a few slight detailed changes, the Aston Martin was transformed into the lithe 282bhp DB5. This was the car chosen for James Bond in *Goldfinger* (Guy Hamilton, 1964) as modified by production designer Ken Adam with ejector seat, machine guns and other cunning devices. The film was hugely successful; so was the car. It was very many little boys' dream car, and doubtless, little girls', too.

193

1973 FORD MUSTANG

A 1970s American dream summed up in one simple snap. Sunshine, a pretty girl in groovy outfit at once body-hugging, and flared like the car, and a Mustang to get away in.

191

192

193

194

194
1949 AEROCAR

Yes, it really can fly. Here is a dream come true, but one that never took off in commercial terms. Perhaps this is just as well. Can you imagine the sky full of pilots who have difficulty driving a stock Chevrolet? Mott Taylor's Lycoming-powered Aerocar remains a wonder. This is no nutty professor's daydream and the engineering is thorough. The glass-fibre-bodied car, which can run on the road at up to 67mph, can be converted into a plane in just five minutes. The car carries it wings folded up behind it on a trailer. Wings in place, up she goes, able to cruise at 100mph-plus for 300 miles. As late as 1970, Ford expressed an interest in mass-producing an aerocar, but nothing happened. Just as 99.99 per cent of cars will never fly, except accidentally, we are not all born to be pilots.

195
1988 FLYING CAR

Here's another way. Stick wings on your Ford Capri, and it's up, up and away.

196
1999 MOLLER M200X

Flying saucers are usually only ever seen in the United States. This is either because aliens prefer to take their holiday there rather than in Uzbekhistan or because they have unwittingly witnessed flights by Dr Paul Miller's M200X flying saucer car. This first flew in 1989, and has since made more than 200 short trips. Today, Muller International is hoping to have its vertical take-off M400 Skycar, a *Star Wars* fighter lookalike, on the market for about $600,000 in 2006. Commuting will never be the same.

195

196

197

198

197 + 198
1936 STOUT SCARAB

Only six or nine – no one seems
sure – of these streamlined,
rear-engined, aluminium-bodied
cars were built between 1936
and 1939. They were remarkable
machines with generous interiors
that could be re-arranged
ingeniously. The engine was a
reliable 100hp Ford flat-head 221
cubic inch V8. The Scarab boasted
all-round coil-spring independent
suspension, and handled pretty
well. It was designed by William B
Stout (1880–1956), inventor, aviator
and one-time editor of *Motor Age*.
It must have looked very odd at the
time – an American equivalent of
the Volkswagen, although the two
machines were developed entirely
independently – and failed to
sell. Shame.

199
1934 DYMAXION III

Designed by the American
engineer, inventor,
environmentalist and sage,
Buckminster Fuller (1895–1983)
wanted to mass-produce a car
using ideas, materials and
technology from the aircraft
industry. The result was the
sci-fi-style Dymaxion. These three
prototype aluminium-bodied 10-
seaters were powered by a rear-
mounted Ford V8 that drove the
two front wheels, while the single
rear wheel steered. "Bucky" made
all sorts of fantastic claims for the
Dymaxion - it could accelerate to
60mph in three seconds, it had
a top speed of 120mph – but
although it rode well in a straight
line, the Dymaxion shied away
from tricky things, like bends. An
accident involving the prototype
and the death of an enthusiastic
English visitor ensured that Fuller
never got the funding he needed to
develop this glorious failure. He
did, though, go on to invent the
geodesic dome and remains a hero
among architects, designers and
imaginative engineers.

200
1958 FORD EDSEL CITATION

It was meant to be the big V8 Ford that everyone wanted. Market research had proved it before the car had turned a wheel. The Edsel was one of Ford's rare flops, and a big one: it sold fewer than half the numbers expected. What the styling department in Detroit was on when they shaped that infamous grille, we will never know. Still, Edsel himself knew more than a little about excess. He asked Albert Kahn, the architect of Ford's Detroit factories, to design him a lakeside home in the English Cotswolds style. It added up to a 60-room mansion stuffed with English and French antiques, and several rooms filled with works by Matisse, Cezanne, Franz Hals and Diego Rivera. Since Edsel died in 1943, there would have been no '58 Citation in his garage. The house, in Macomb County, Michigan is open to the public.

201
1975 VANDEN PLAS 1500

A posh limousine, a miniature Austin Princess for everyman, this is the Vanden Plas 1500, one of the most delightfully pretentious cars of all time. Based on the curious, boiled-sweet shaped Austin Allegro, the 1500cc front-wheel-drive saloon boasted a luxurious leather and walnut-veneered interior and a Bentley-style grille. Originally a Belgian supplier to the early motor industry and then a coachbuilder to such illustrious marques as Rolls-Royce, Alvis and Lagonda, the British arm of Vanden Plas, was founded in 1913 and became a subsidiary of Austin in 1946. The Kingsbury works in north London closed in 1979 and Vanden Plas became nothing more than a smart name. The 1500 model is much prized in Japan as an example of English eccentricity. The first popular model to get the Vanden Plas treatment was an 1963 Issigonis-designed Austin 1100 done up in leather and walnut for Fred Connolly, leather supplier to the motor industry. It was much admired – so much so that Austin put it into production. The Japanese collect this endearing model, too.

202
1975 AMC PACER

Long before most mass-production cars began to look like half-sucked boiled sweets, Richard A Teague (1923–91) designed the blobby Pacer for AMC (swallowed up by Chrysler in 1987). It was wide, spacious and not as bad as it was made out to be by those who found its shape hard to swallow. Just 280,000 sold between 1975 and 1980 – chicken-feed in the US – and few survive. Originally it was to have included several advanced engineering features, including a rotary Wankel engine, but in the end it was pretty conventional. It looked, said too many for the car's good, like a frog or a pregnant guppy.

201

202

CARS AND SEX

203

203
1917 OLDSMOBILE
The world is at war, but you would never guess from this charming portrait of an American beauty modelling a white silk dress on the running board of a gleaming '17 Oldsmobile.

204
1955 FIAT 1400 SALOON AND 1100 103TV TRASFORMABILE
Most people wear blue overalls at oil refineries, but not this Italian model who has chosen a tightly fitted coat and fur stole – on a sunny day, too. This fashion shot was taken in Milan in 1955. The cars are brand new, although the pretty 50hp Trasformabile, with its shark-nose grille and wrap-round windscreen, looks decidedly more modern than the stolid, taxi-style 1400 alongside. Cars were much used in fashion magazines in the 1950s and 1960s.

205

205

1956 GOGGOMOBIL T300

Go on, guess who the leopard skin model is… Jackie Collins, author of *The Stud* (1969), *The Bitch* (1979) and *Deadly Embrace* (2002) no less. While glamorous Jackie has gone on to sell more than 200 million books, the Goggomobil has fared less well. In fact, the Hans Glas's car company was taken over by BMW in 1969. Jackie is sitting in what appears to be a special luxury edition of the 15hp, 293cc 95km/h German saloon. She will move on to better things 12 years later when she publishes her first best-seller *The World is Full of Married Men* (1968), but few Goggomobiles.

206

1957 SIMCA ARONDE

There we were, Monsieur le Gendarme, just driving back from the ball and suddenly half the *voiture*, how you say, vanished. A strange episode from the 1957 Paris motor show featuring two belles in extravagant frocks and half a car. Would such grande dames really have chosen a humble Simca?

207

1964 ASTON MARTIN DB5

Here's some real English-style glamour: leggy bottle blonde, gloriously seedy backdrop – ladder, plank, assorted junk – with one of the sexiest cars ever looking good despite every attempt to reduce it to the level of a prop in a *Carry On* film. The DB5 remains one of the most coveted of all British cars.

206

207

208

208
1966 FIAT BERTONE SHOW CAR
Slight lapse of taste here on the Bertone show stand. The model looks decidedly uncomfortable in a huge, busby-like wig and bizarrely engineered bikini. Still, she hides the car, which is clearly not one of the great carrozeria's best.

209
1969 GP RACER
'Allo, dahlin'. Sheer, sex-sational class, innit, at the British Grand Prix, 1969. A fast, sticky lady, perhaps, but not quite so fast as the slippery Jackie Stewart, who won the race in a Matra MS80.

209

210

210
1968 FIAT 124 SPIDER
Car turns into model who turns into car. Peggy Walton, a model at the 1968 New York motor show, seems all but indistinguishable from the pretty Fiat Spider. A funny, and almost innocent, image.

211
1987 TVR-ES
Fast, eye-catching, blowsy and loud, TVRs are built in Blackpool, Lancashire. Here car and motor show models are in perfect accord.

212
1988 PANTHER KALLISTA
Tasteful, or what?

213
1999 TOYOTA AXV CONCEPT CAR
Sometimes, we are all stumped for words. This is very possibly Toyota's homage to the Spice Girls. Or not. Tokyo motor show, 1999.

211

212

213

214
1955 BMW ISETTA
Hopping one-legged style from a German bubble car. It might have been a fashionable pose, or was it just cramp? Natty outfit matched by the car's stylish tartan upholstery.

215
1960 TOYOTA TIARA
Model Diane Chiljan jacks up one of the new 75hp Nipponse sedans aimed squarely at the US market; she splits her skirt in the process. Women and cars, I ask you…

216
1956 BOND TYPE-D MINICAR
Here's lovely would-be debutante Gay McGregor reversing the 197cc '56 Bond across a swirly carpet at the three-wheeler's debut at a London hotel. That year's Suez Crisis, when Britain unwisely attempted to invade Egypt, led to a steep rise in the price of petrol. A parsimonious Bond made some sense. Bet the charming Miss McGregor with her Sussex teashop smile didn't own one, though.

214

215

217

**1963 HILLMAN MINX
CONVERTIBLE**
Fetching sleeveless dress in pink
or blue and white checked cotton
with collar and pussy-cat bow
in white organdie. By Bernshaw.
Modelled by fetching gal smoking
a fag in squishy 1,494cc Minx.

218
1969 US MUSCLE CAR
"A driving outfit designed for
long or short trips in the summer
season." Flares are back, in
2003, but whatever happened
to driving outfits?

219

219
1955 FORD POPULAR
Blimey, mush, cop a load of that, and no mistake! Cockney geezer, circa 1960, gets pumped with gallons of free petrol from a Barbara-Windsor-style dolly bird. This image is either very funny or rather sad. Still, the MoT test is only a year away at best and the Popular may well be off the road for good, while our bikini clad lovely might be able to buy some clothes before she catches a death as the British economy picks up.

220
1954 FORD CONSUL MK1
Almost impossibly English scene. Charming schoolgirls in bikinis – Stella Long, Marilyn Woolhead and Karen Lewis – buff, polish and prod some battered and wonderfully dumpy gor'blimey Ford at a petrol station at Ealing, west London as part of a publicity campaign by English Petroleum in November 1965. That's right, November, a good month in England to prance about in bathing costumes.

221
1954 DAIMLERS
Here's Lady Norah Docker in a modest and tasteful white satin number embroidered with sequins depicting hubby's Daimler cars. The occasion is a fancy dress ball at the Poole Harbour Yacht Club in January 1954. The policeman is Lady Norah's son, Lance.

222
1954 DAIMLER STARDUST
M'lady Docker in furs, attracting press attention in the plush salon of her '54 Daimler. Rationing was just coming to an end in Austerity-era post-war Britain when this fetching snap was taken. Although extravagant and decidedly camp, the former Norah Collins – a one-time dancer at London's Café de Paris – was a popular figure during the years her husband, Bernard Docker, was chairman of Daimler. She added greatly to the gaiety of the nation in glum, monochrome times.

222

220

221

222

223
1954 JOE DIMAGGIO'S CAR
Marilyn Monroe leaves her
Beverly Hills home in tears,
with baseball star husband Joe
Dimaggio at the vast wheel of
their slinky car. Marilyn was about
to sue for divorce. She knew how
to look good for the cameras even
in times of distress.

224
**c 1960 MARILYN MONROE
LIMOUSINE**
Making a cute and knowing
automotive exit with next husband,
Arthur Miller.

225
1956 FORD THUNDERBIRD
American dream. Marilyn Monroe
and Arthur Miller setting off
for a picnic from their Roxbury,
Connecticut home on June 30,
1956, the day after their wedding.
Marilyn starred with Don Murray in
Joshua Logan's *Bus Stop* that year.
Miller had achieved international
fame as a playwright with his
Death of a Saleman (1949). The
happy couple divorced in 1961, the
year John Huston's *Misfits* starred
Monroe at perhaps her very best
and with a taut screenplay by Miller.

223

224

226

1962 RENAULT CARAVELLE S
The divine Brigitte Bardot and two pets in St Tropez in 1962: a dachshund and a rear-engined, 956cc Renault Caravelle S. The Renault was a bit like the VW Karmann-Ghia: not fast, but lithe and gently voluptuous. BB, however, was definitely more than a match for both. She had promoted Renault cars from 1960.

227

228

227
1955 SUNBEAM ALPINE TOURER
Here's Grace Kelly with Cary Grant on location on the French Riviera during the filming of *To Catch a Thief* (Alfred Hitchcock, 1955). The British director said she had "sexual elegance", and who would say Hitch was wrong? This was when the beautiful actress met her future husband, Prince Rainier III, at the Cannes Film Festival. She became Princess Grace of Monaco the following year. She died in Monte Carlo on September 14, 1982 at the wheel of her Rover 3500. She was said to have suffered a stroke; the car plunged 45 feet from a twisting cliff road.

228
1959 CADILLAC FLEETWOOD
This windy picture is from Gina Lollobrigida's family album, dated January 1, 1970. Nice to see a '59 Caddie getting the glamorous star treatment years on from its sensational debut. "La Lollo" was one of European cinema's first post-war sex symbols. She starred in dozens of films in both Italy and the US in the 1950s and 1960s. She is also a talented photo-journalist as *Italia Mia* (1973), her first book of photographs, amply proved.

229
1968 TRIUMPH SPITFIRE
I say, look at that cracking 1,296cc engine, chaps! Much bigger than the previous 1,147cc unit, eh? Standard-issue British men ignore standard-issue British blonde.

230
1998 MINI
Cheery mini-skirted blondes, free from the attention, or lack of it, of standard-issue British men, click-clack past one of the very last new Issigonis Minis. The Mini was a mechanical cherub, cheeky if never exactly sexy.

231
1998 JORDAN GP RACER
Jordan, the saucy 34FF tabloid model astride the priapic nose of a Jordan at the 1998 Spanish Grand Prix. The team did well that year, with Damon Hill and Ralf Schumacher coming home 1-2 at the Belgian Grand Prix. Jordan – Katie Price – went on to much bigger things, standing for parliament as candidate for the Greater Manchester constituency of Stretford and Urmiston on a "free plastic surgery for all ticket". She didn't win, but continued to wow paparazzi, footballers, sticky schoolboys and the 'ello darlin' British tabloid press.

CARS AS STARS

232
1959 MERCEDES-BENZ 190SL
Alfred Hitchcock, at the height of his powers, and at the wheel of his Merc leaving the MGM studios after a day's work on his classic thriller *North by North West* (1959), starring Cary Grant and James Mason.

233

233

233
1959 MERCEDES-BENZ 190SL
Here's Yul Brynner, in 1959, off for a spin in his 190SL, clearly very fashionable that year in Hollywood. No time to change out of his costume; he was starring in *Solomon and Sheb* (King Vidor, 1959) alongside Gina Lollobrigida at the time.

234
1963 ASTON MARTIN DB5
Sean Connery, the perfect James Bond, poses with the gadget-laden *Goldfinger* DB5; the car was a perfect match for Connery's iron-fist-in-velvet-glove film persona.

234

234

235
1964 US "STOCK" CAR
Elvis and Ann-Margaret looking utterly cool and unfazed at speed in the Nevada desert as Lucky Jackson and Rusty Martin in a sporting number in a scene from *Viva Las Vegas* (George Sidney, 1964).

235

236

237

236+237
1954 PORSCHE 550

James Byron Dean came to a nasty end on September 30, 1955 when he smashed his lightweight (550kg) racing Porsche near the intersection of highways 41 and 46 at Cholame, California. He was 24 years old and an up-and-coming Hollywood star. The car was just one of 78 sold to the public. One of his fellow actors in *Rebel Without a Cause* (Nicholas Ray, 1955) was Beverly Long. Later, she said of a ride in the fated car with Dean, "I felt like I was riding in a tombstone. I had never ridden in a Porsche. And when you sit down, you sit down. And you feel like you're on the ground. I had the feeling I was sitting in a coffin. It was very scary. And Jimmy drove way too fast." The Porsche was designed with a cause, to win its class at Le Mans, which it did in 1954. It also won the classic Targa Florio, driven by Umberto Maglioli, in 1956. Designed by Wilhelm Hild and bodied by Weidenhusen of Frankfurt, it had a top speed of 220km/h. It was not, despite its looks, a "toy." James Dean called it his "Little Bastard." But that depended on how this fierce and brilliant little car was driven.

238
1966 AC COBRA 427

Carrol Shelby first fitted the tough, chuckable British AC Ace sports car with a mighty, high-revving, seven-litre Ford V8. The result was a blistering racing car and one of the fastest accelerating road cars of all time. Elvis got to drive one on *Spinout* (Norman Taurog, 1966). Pursued not just by other racing cars, but also by three pouting lovelies determined to race him up to the altar, Elvis stays loyal to his Cobra. The advertising blurb screamed, "It's Elvis with his foot on the gas and no brakes on the fun!!!" Hmm. The cars are great, but with songs like "Adam and Evil" and, I kid you not, "Smorgasbord", *Spinout* seems to have spun off the classic movie circuit. ACs are still made to thrill at Thames Ditton in Surrey.

239
1918 MODEL-T FORD
Hollywood's silent stars got a lot of laughs smashing up horseless carriages. Here's the great, deadpan comedian Buster Keaton (1895–1966) typically unfazed as the Tin Lizzie driven by Fatty Arbuckle (1887–1933) collapses in front of a Hollywood garage.

240
1954 AUSTIN J40
This is Norman Wisdom (b 1915), an English comedian popular in the 1950s who went on to become a star in Romania in later years – the brutal Communist dictator, Nicolae Ceausescu found him funny. However, he did remarkably well as a serious actor in later life. In this chase scene from *One Good Turn* (John Carstairs, 1954), Wisdom is driving an Austin Junior Forty pedal car. These delightful toys – all 32,098 of them – were made by Austin in a factory at Bargoed in South Wales by disabled coal miners, from 1949 to 1971. Originally, they cost £33 and were based on the design of the 1948 Austin A40 Devon. A working horn and headlamps were included in the price. Later, the factory made components for the long-lived BMC/Leyland/Mini A-series engine, until its closure in 1999.

240

241

1969 MINI COOPER S
The real stars of *The Italian Job* (Peter Collinson, 1969) were not Michael Caine, Noel Coward, Benny Hill or even the wonderful Fred Emney and John Le Mesurier, but the cars. There were a lot of these. They included not just a trio of brilliantly driven Cooper S Minis ricocheting through Turin, but a Lamborghini Miura, Aston Martin DB6 Volante, a pair of E-Type Jags, a Series 1 Land Rover, Fiat Dino Coupes (the Mafia), Alfa Romeo Giulias (the police) and a triple-axled Bedford Legionnaire coach that steals the final scene. Here, one of the Minis is seen interrupting a wedding, while all three are caught squealing along the *terrazo* floors of one of Turin's magnificent nineteenth century arcades. A forthcoming American remake of the film stars three of the new and much brawnier BMW Minis, although 32 have been used, and abused, in the actual making of the movie.

1977 LOTUS ESPRIT S1

The Lotus Esprit epitomizes much of 1970s car design. The cheese-wedge shape, a cabin fitted out in carpet, recessed door handles… and yet it is still a Lotus, which spells superb peformance, razor-sharp handling and a certain rakish charm. It seemed just the car for an updated James Bond. Now that Roger Moore had replaced Sean Connery in the 007 role, it was decided that he ought to have a car of his own. In reality the Lotus Esprit Series 1 was neither as fast nor as furious as it looks suggested. It was powered by a two-litre, twin-cam four that gave 160bhp – not enough to keep up with the Porsche 911 and Ferrari 308, its intended rivals. Bond's version in the hugely successful *The Spy Who Loved Me* (Lewis Gilbert, 1977) was able to turn into a submarine to escape villains. Ken Adam, the production designer, says that several standard road cars were used in the filming as well as two submarine body shells. One of the cars was simply shot by a water cannon into the water. A second had retractable wheels so that these could be filmed in close-up, while the third was a genuine submersible piloted by a stuntman in a scuba-diving outfit. The aerodynamics of the Esprit's shape meant that the sub kept nosing downwards – downforce, useful on the road, was no help at all in water – and even scraping the bottom. Roger Moore, surrounded by fans and extras on a beach, looks, of course, as cool, as dry and as unstirred as a vodka Martini.

244

244
1968 DODGE CHARGER 440

This is the villains' car in *Bullitt* (Peter Yates, 1968), the classic 1960s car chase thriller, starring Steve McQueen and set in San Francisco. The undoubted highlight of the film was the dice to the death between McQueen's 1968 Ford Mustang GT390 and the equally brutal, Coke-bottle style Dodge Charger. The cars were driven very much for real – no digital sequences then – at speeds of up to 110mph on real streets. Bud Elkins was the Mustang's stunt driver, while Bill Hickman drove the Dodge. McQueen did some of his own driving, but it wasn't easy. A third vehicle in the chase, which, of course, you never see was the camera car, a sort of sawn-off Corvette.

245
1981 PLYMOUTH FURY/ DODGE DIPLOMAT

"Hill Street Blues", a long-running and hugely popular NBC cop show – 146 episodes between 1981 and 1987 – was a showcase for a variety of leaping, screeching, squealing squad cars. The V8-powered Fury and the Diplomat featured among others. These vast, ship-like cars could take a lot of punishment, and often did, in the hands of Captain Frank Furillo's finest, from Hill Street Station.

246 + 247
1959 RENAULT 4CV

More than a million of these little Renaults were built between 1947 and 1961. Designed by Fernard Picard using as few (at that time) precious materials as possible, prototypes were tested in total secrecy from 1942. Its bug-like profile was much liked. The 760cc car was easy to drive, friendly and reliable. The public nicknamed it "puce", or "pet", so it was fascinating to see it cast in a villainous role in Jean-Luc Godard's cult film *A bout de souffle* (Breathless) of 1959. A young hoodlum, played by Jean-Paul Belmondo, steals a car and drives to Paris. He finds a gun in the car and shoots dead the motorcycle cop who tries to stop him. The film is full off fascinating economy model French cars of the 1950s. It also stars the gamine Jean Seberg, who we see running the gauntlet between a Renault Dauphine, the 4CV's successor.

245

246

247

248

1949 MERCURY

James Dean made two cars famous – the Porsche 550 he died in and the '49 Mercury V8 he drove in the cult teenage angst classic *Rebel Without a Cause* (Nicholas Ray, 1955). The Mercury, which looked like an inverted bath tub, was actually a quick and capable car; it could top 100mph and boasted independent front suspension, so could wobble around corners better than many less sophisticated contemporaries. It was also a car that young Americans enjoyed hotting-up; the style of the car took to this well. They remain much sought-after classics today. In this publicity shot for the film, the driver's window seems the wrong profile for a Mercury, but, hell, that's the car our Jimmy drove.

249

1961 FERRARI 250GT CALIFORNIA

In *Ferris Bueller's Day Off* (John Hughes, 1986), this superb Scaglietti-bodied Ferrari appears to have a very rough time, at one point shooting through a sheet of plate glass. Not to worry. Four replicas were made for the film by Modena Design and Development, El Cajon, California. These five-litre Ford V8 replicars may not have the ultimate cachet of a multi-cog-spinning V12 Ferrari, but you would have to be exceptionally keen eyed to spot the difference on film. The Californian-built cars are not allowed to carry the prized Ferrari leaping horse badge. That's how you tell, unless you raise the hood.

250

1971 PORSCHE 917

Among the all-time great racing cars, the Porsche 917 was a formidable 250mph beast that trounced all opposition in its Le Mans heyday. Steve McQueen drove a Gulf-Porsche 917 fast and well in *Le Mans* (Lee H Katzin, 1971), his sequences, and those of other professional drivers hired for the film, cut in and out of footage of the real 1970 event when 917s came home 1-2-3. Driving in the film was full-on; one driver lost a leg when he crashed. The 917 was powered a truly Teutonic 4.5-litre (later five-litre) flat 12 that cranked out between 580bhp (1969) and 1,560bhp (1973, 917/30). The racing rule books were rewritten for 1974 to keep the 917 out of the picture and the all-conquering machine was forced to retire. Do not even attempt to watch the film unless you like fast, powerful cars. There is not much else in it.

251

1961 FORD THUNDERBIRD

This 300bhp, lipstick-red tearaway was a perfect mobile prop for Susan Sarandon and Gina Davis, stars of the feminist road movie *Thelma and Louise* (Ridley Scott, 1991). If ever a car suggests "freedom of the road", this it it.

252

1963 VOLKSWAGEN BEETLE

Car Number 53, where are you? Right on top of your head, buddy. This is Herbie in action. The Bug starred in four cute Disney films as well as a duff TV series. It was a neat idea to take a car that can barely top 80mph and turn it into a child-friendly supercar. There are some delightful parodies of other films and Herbie's antics are amusing. The four films were *The Love Bug* (1969), *Herbie Rides Again* (1974), *Herbie Goes to Monte Carlo* (1977) and *Herbie Goes Bananas* (1980).

248

250

249

251

252

254

253
1966 BATMOBILE

Holy Ford, Batman! This was really the $250,000 1955 Lincoln Futura concept car in cartoon-style disguise. Originally designed by Bill Schmidt, after an encounter with a real life shark, the shark-like car was bodied by Ghia and toured the US until its retirement in 1959. It popped up again in *It Started with a Kiss* (George Marshall, 1959) starring Debbie Reynolds and Glen Ford. In 1966 it was converted – in just three weeks before filming began – into the Batmobile by George Barris for ABC's new "Batman" series. Batman (Adam West) and Robin (Burt Ward) camped about happily in the intentionally funny Bam! Pow! Pop! shows, and made the Batmobile a star with children everywhere. A number of plastic replicas were made during the series, which ran until 1968; a custom car expert, George Barris owns the original, steel-bodied car.

254
1962 VOLVO P1800

Leslie Charteris's fictional hero, Simon Templar aka The Saint, drove an equally fictional Hirondel. When the story was made into a TV series, "The Saint", in 1962, Jaguar refused an E-Type, much to its later regret – the programme was extremely popular and ran for years – and Volvo drove in with a white 115bhp P1800. This was never the fastest or most dynamic sports car; in fact it was hardly a sports car at all. But it looked good. Four cars were supplied over the years, including one for Roger Moore's personal use. The 1964 car, 77 GYL, is on permanent show at the Cars of the Stars Museum, Keswick, England. For the first two years of its life, the P1800 was assembled by Jensen in West Bromwich, England; production was transferred to Gothenburg in 1963.

255
1975 FORD GRAN TORINO

The cops-chase-robbers "Starsky and Hutch" TV series starring David Soul and Paul Glaser had such a cult following that, for 1976, Ford issued a special line of 1,000 tomato red and white-striped Starsky and Hutch Gran Torinos. A case of life imitating art. The TV car had a 400 cubic inch V8 under the hood and was fast.

256
1969 DODGE CHARGER

Bo, Luke and Daisy's mount in the "Dukes of Hazzard" was General Lee, a customized, bright orange '69 Dodge Charger that did a lot of charging around Hazzard County, set, fictionally, in Georgia. Filming of the car chase TV series was split between Georgia and California. Great fun. Fun car.

255

256

257

257
1965 ROLLS-ROYCE PHANTOM V
Delivered new to John Lennon in June 1965, this Mulliner Park Ward bodied Phantom V was originally painted glossy black. In April 1967, while making "Sergeant Pepper's Lonely Heart's Club Band", Lennon took the car to J P Fallon Ltd, a Chertsey coachbuilder. For about £2,000, the car was painted in swirls and swags of flowers by a team of Dutch gypsy artists called The Fool. Lennon took the car to New York in 1970 where he lent it, variously, to the Rolling Stones, Moody Blues and Bob Dylan. Donated to the Cooper-Hewitt Museum, New York, in 1977 in exchange for a $225,000 tax credit, the car is now preserved in the Ottowa Museum of Science and Technology.

258
1960s ROLLS-ROYCES
A trio of Rolls-Royces outside Elstree Studios in February 1969, where Tom Jones was recording his ABC-TV series "This is Tom Jones". Jones (left) sits astride his 1966 "Chinese Eyes" Silver Cloud III (you could get away with labels like that in the politically incorrect 1960s) and the 1966 Silver Shadow of his manager, Gordon Mills. On the right with his 1965 Phantom V is singer Engelbert Humperdinck. The boys had done good.

259
1966 PONTIAC GTO
Here they come, driving down the street, getting funniest looks from everyone that they meet. No surprise when four gurning young men are leaning out of a highly customized Pontiac. This car, the Monkeemobile, was one of two created by Dean Jeffries. It featured three rows of seats, a parachute and, originally, a blower that allowed the cars to perform spectacular wheelies. Wisely, this was removed. The Monkees – Mike Nesmith, Peter Tork, Micky Dolenz and Davy Jones – were each given a stock '66 GTO by Pontiac. Nice work if you can get it. One of the Monkeemobiles is now owned by George Barris, creator of the Batmobile.

258

The publishers would like to thank the following sources for their kind permission to reproduce the pictures in this book:

The Advertising Archive Ltd.: 166M, 166R, 167, 173L, 174L, 174M, 174R, 176, 177
Action Images: Brandon Malone: 229
Album Archivo Fotografico: Paramount Pictures/Cortesía Album: 240; /Solar/Cinema Center/ Cortesía Album: 246BR
Auto Express Picture Library: 118
BMW (GB) Ltd.: 95, 130B, 130M, 228B
Michael Cooper: 54, 55
Corbis Images: 33TR, 90, 97T, 98B, 99, 101, 109, 136; /Paul Almasy: 151; /Bettmann: 24, 25L, 47, 51, 52-53, 91, 93, 96B, 102, 103, 110, 126, 150, 157, 194L, 194R, 202, 210, 216T, 219R, 224L, 224R, 225, 226, 234, 235BR, 235TR, 248; /Sheldan Collins: 85B; /Hulton-Deutsch Collection: 9T, 50, 64, 65B, 98M, 98T, 106, 130T, 144, 145, 188, 212, 213BL, 213BR, 222B, 222T, 250T; /Lake County Museum: 156BL; /Lester Lefkowitz: 143; /Lollobrigida Gina: 227ML; /London Aerial Photo Library: 142; /Jerry Ohlinger: 227TL; /PEMCO - Webster & Stevens Collection; Museum of History & Industry, Seattle: 163; /Flip Schulke: 104, 105; /Sean Sexton Collection: 92; /Studio Patellani: 211; / Swim Ink: 162; /John Swope Collection: 125; /Peter Turnley: 111;/ Tom Wagner: 217; /Roger Wood: 8
Daimler Chrysler: 40, 42, 52TL, 82
Detroit Public Library: 30T, 40T, 74L, 74R, 75, 77, 81B, 81T, 83, 94B, 95T, 120M, 129, 184, 185, 186, 187, 189, 191, 192, 193, 197, 198B, 198M, 198T, 199, 200, 202BL
Fiat Auto UK Ltd.: 80L, 122
Ford Motor Company: 80R, 107, 235MR; /From the collections of Henry Ford Museum/Greenfield Village: 9B, 25T, 34B, 137
General Motors: 10, 26B, 28, 30B, 33TL, 43B, 43T, 66L, 66R, 195T
Getty Images: Jeff Gross: 58-59; /Robert Laberge: 56B; /Bryn Lennon: 57
Rosetta Graham: 4, 11
Hulton Archive: 67, 116, 119B, 123, 124, 138-39, 140, 141, 146-47, 148, 152R, 154, 155T, 156B, 182, 190, 195B, 218L, 219, 220, 221, 238
Jaguar: 13, 196
The Kobal Collection: 249MR; /MGM/Pathe: 246BR; /Hal Roach/MGM: 35; /Universal: 244B; /Warner Bros: 244T
Gideon Mendel: 60, 112
Motoring Picture Library: 14B, 14T, 15L, 15R, 18, 28, 31, 32, 33BR, 40BL, 44L, 44R, 45, 48B, 48T, 49, 56T, 68, 72B, 72T, 73, 76, 79, 84, 119T, 120B, 120T, 121, 127B, 127T, 128L, 128R, 165, 168, 169, 170, 175, 183, 202ML, 204, 214, 215, 216B, 216M, 205BL, 205BR, 228T
Pal Negyesi: 78
Peugeot: 34T
Photos12.com: 26T, 27, 40M, 92, 201L; /Bertelsmann Lexikon Verlag: 69; /Citroën: 65T; /Collection Cinema: 239, 245ML, 245MR, 246BL, 246TL; /Hached: 100; /Keystone Pressedienst: 70, 152L; /Oasis: 96T
Private Collection: 6, 17, 18T, 20, 36, 60, 86, 132, 158, 172B, 172T, 178, 206, 230
Rex Features: 108L, 111T, 153, 201R, 236ML, 236TL, 237, 241, 242-43, 247, 249BR, 249ML, 251
Penny Simpson: 12
Topham: 16, 97B, 108R, 149, 166L, 223L, 223R, 250B; /Fotomas: 173R; /Imageworks: 85T; /National Motor Museum: 46, 117, 164, 171B, 171T

Endpaper Credits:

Corbis/Bettmann, Hulton Archive and General Motors

Every effort has been made to acknowledge correctly and contact the source and/or copyright holder of each picture, and Carlton Books Limited apologises for any unintentional errors, or omissions, which will be corrected in future editions of this book.